GOD CAN'T FIX \

M000013273

Disassembly
Required

Tyeisha Crutchfield

Trilogy Christian Publishers
A Wholly Owned Subsidiary of Trinity Broadcasting Network
2442 Michelle Drive
Tustin, CA 92780

For information, address Trilogy Christian Publishing
Rights Department, 2442 Michelle Drive, Tustin, Ca 92780.
Trilogy Christian Publishing/ TBN and colophon are trademarks
of Trinity Broadcasting Network.
For information about special discounts for bulk purchases,
please contact Trilogy Christian Publishing.
Manufactured in the United States of America

10 9 8 7 6 5 4 3 2 1
Library of Congress Cataloging-in-Publication Data is available.
ISBN 978-1-64773-819-8
ISBN 978-1-64773-820-4 (ebook)

DEDICATION

This book is dedicated to my Mom, Nicole L. Meads.

It's hard to write about everything that's wrong with you. What makes it even harder is knowing that my brokenness came from voids in my life, which overshadows the one person who was present in my life and consistently pouring into me. Although words won't be able to express, I'll say it anyway: my mom is my world and did more good in my life than this book will mention or I can ever repay. She is the reason I stand not crushed by my journey but able to testify about it so that others may be healed. Thank you, mom; I owe you everything.

ACKNOWLEDGEMENTS

I'd like to give special thanks to Elevation Church in Charlotte, NC where I was able to find relationship with Jesus, discover His love for me, and find community and solid direction. And to Pastor Mike Todd of Transformation Church in Tulsa, OK. My second pastor and a guiding light through my journey. His sermon "Marked" preached at Elevation in 2018 jumpstarted my journey to purpose and his series Relationship Goals and All Strings Attached gave me the power and knowledge I needed to be committed to this new relationship and wade through the journey. You'll see a lot of quotes and references to sermons from them, because they were both instrumental in my journey. Thank you.

TABLE OF CONTENTS

INTRODUCTION

break₁
/brāk/

verb

1. separate or cause to separate into pieces as a result
    of a blow, shock, or strain.

The common view of the healing process is that
something is coming together or mending. Not so
in the story of my life. My healing happened by breaking.

The idea of breaking typically has a negative context. If something or someone breaks, it's not whole
anymore, but rather pieces of the thing you once owned
and probably loved. To most people, those pieces will
likely seem useless and they'll be tossed out. Or, some
may try to glue the pieces back together in an attempt

to recreate the picture they once had. Every single synonym for the word "break" or "broken" has a negative connotation; one of which is to be damaged, which has a permanent emphasis. But what if breaking wasn't a bad thing? What if it was a necessary process to create the originally intended picture? That would insinuate that the picture you previously had wasn't right, wouldn't it? What if that picture was your life, and you're being broken? And what if that's a good thing?

What if the only way to heal, was to break? Would you submit to that? That would change the very nature of how we view broken things, wouldn't it? So much so that we might actually give in to the breaking process, knowing that it's for our good. Knowing that something good, something right, is to come from the pieces.

I had the honor of being broken by God. I don't know what blow, shock, or strain forced this process into action, but it did, and I'm grateful. To say it was an honor sounds cheesy, over the top, and a little unnecessary, but I don't know how else to describe it. God allowed me to endure this painful process of breaking without giving up. And He allowed me to see the beauty in the separation while being disassembled.

There are no experts of life. Tons of experts in the world that exhaust the knowledge of specific subjects but none who are experts of life. The only people who could potentially be an expert on life are people who can say "been there, done that" and can say that they finished the race. Those people are dead. There will always be living people who you can learn from, but the true experts, they're not here anymore. I said that to say, I don't claim to be an expert; I claim to have had an experience. And that's what I want to share; my experience of breaking as God's intended process for healing.

So, a little about me. I'm in my late 20's and I live a simple, stable life. I graduated magna cum laude from undergrad and immediately got started with my career in marketing at 22 years old. I've been in marketing ever since, working for national and international brands. Promotion after promotion, raise after raise, I worked my butt off to become who I saw myself becoming when I was a teenager. For someone my age, I was doing pretty well for myself in my career from an earthly perspective. I also started pursuing my MBA right out of undergrad. After 4 years of little to no progression in that degree, I switched to pursuing a degree in theology in 2018. I now have my Master's in Theological Studies. I bought my first house at 28 (first in my family to do so). I serve at my local church, and gosh I love Jesus with all of my heart and soul. Model citizen, right? Ha, no. I was your typical social media façade just waiting to be cracked open.

Looking back, I can see how that façade was created. As I was becoming who I thought I was supposed to be, my past shaped me, new knowledge developed me, and new experiences opened my eyes. Little did I know, what I was building was a mirage, sort of like a 1,000-piece puzzle that you put together all wrong. The pieces might fit as you build it out but, at some point, you realize that in the way the pieces are put together, they don't form the picture on the front of the box. Or, you see that it might slightly resemble the right picture, but not really in the way it was intended to. Let me paint a picture for you....

I saw this on social media one day with the caption "Did I do it right?" and man did this describe the first 25ish years of my life SOO perfectly. I mean, the person clearly tried and to be honest, it's not a bad picture. It resembles the picture on the box, the colors appear to be in the right place, and I can see a clear image with what they've put together. It's a picture and it's doing a pretty good job of mimicking the example given but simply not put together right, or at all for that matter. That picture was my life. There were directions and a right way to do things, even a guiding example; but I put pieces where I thought they belonged just to get something in formation. I just wanted some form of a picture. But it wasn't the picture that came on the box. And the result was that I was left with a distorted image that should have been a masterpiece after all of the time it took to put together.

And see, the thing about a puzzle that God manufactured is that the pieces won't sit content in your version of a picture. They will yell at you, consistently, until they're put in the right places. So, as a child of God, you can't just be content with the fact that your picture is put together if you know in your heart it's not put together right. Everything in you fights that contentment until you take action and move towards the picture that God intended to have. I couldn't have peace knowing that the picture of my life was so distorted. On the outside, I was living the dream. On the inside, there were holes, there was damage and there were so many pieces missing. I couldn't find real joy or happiness with my "oh so great life" until I went back to the manufacturer provided image to realign my pieces.

Now, as an almost 30-year-old, I had to begin to

disassemble my puzzle so that I could try to put it together correctly. I have to pull apart everything that I'm made of and reassess where it belongs, or if it belongs at all. I had to start from scratch and hope that I didn't damage any pieces, as I had them forced into the wrong places. Now that I've submitted to the fact that I need to be broken down and taken apart, the mending process begins. You can't fix what's not broken. Through disassembly, through each piece that's being pulled apart, I'm taking one step closer to the originally intended picture. Through the removal of each piece that was lodged into a place that it didn't belong, I'm choosing healing through brokenness. I'm choosing to become a masterpiece by mastering my pieces.

V*oid*

---

void₁
/void/

adjective

1. completely empty.

A void is an empty, unallocated space. Unallocated space was all there was in the world until God breathed life into it (Gen. 1:2, KJV) and it's what we're made up of until God breathes life into us. After we're born with the life that God breathed into us, we await to be filled with love, affection, nurture, and care from the people that He assigned to our lives. We're born needing things that we don't even know we need, depending on people we don't know, and expecting things to happen when we don't know how those things are going to happen. We're born depending on someone else to love us, protect us, and do right by us.

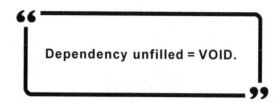

> Dependency unfilled = VOID.

We are dependent by nature. And though we grow up, and eventually figure out how to take care of ourselves, that dependency doesn't go away. As humans, our dependency grows with us, and we just have to understand what we're dependent on. The dependency that we're born with is what creates an opportunity for void to enter in our lives. Dependency unfilled = VOID.

Dependency is such a natural thing; we're born with it from day one, so it's not really acknowledged as a doorway to void. That's not to present dependency as a bad thing; it's the nature that God gave us. But where there is dependency and lack of fulfillment, a void is naturally created. Those voids can be something as simple as hunger. If you need food and you haven't eaten, or if there's nothing around to eat, you become hungry. Or, the void can be as complicated as a baby girl who was born into a single parent home with no father around. That unfulfilled dependency creates a powerful void, a lingering one. That unfulfilled empty space is a sneaky one because the child typically isn't aware that there's even a void, nor does she understand what she's missing. You can't miss what you never had. You don't know what you don't know. It creates an unacknowledged, misunderstood void because something is missing, and the child may act out, but the behavior doesn't always point to the problem. Unlike the hunger that you get with lack of food, with this void, you don't know what you need because you've never had it.

This may sound like the stereotypical story of a father-less child, and I get if that's boring, but this is literally the genetic make-up of my bondage, my experience, and my freedom. This book isn't about my dad or his lack of presence in my life, but the void that he helped create, which was a canvas for me to determine what pieces should live on it. It was the start of my distorted picture.

My dad wasn't around growing up. Children in more than half of the households in our country endure this same experience today, so it may not sound like an obstacle, but it is. It might be the norm, but it wasn't in God's design. Genesis 1:28 says "God blessed them and said to them, 'Be fruitful and increase in number; fill the earth and subdue it'" (NIV). This was after He created male and female in His image. His instruction to them as a unit was to procreate together. There are some households where this situation isn't optional, but when a parent that helped bring a child into the world decides they don't want to give the child what they need and what that child is dependent on, that parent creates a void in that child's life. Regardless of if the child knows it or not, it's unfortunate.

Not only was my dad not around, it was also pretty clear to my mom that he didn't want her to have me. She struggled a lot throughout her pregnancy to maintain sanity knowing that the father of her child didn't want the child to come into this world. She also struggled with people trying to give her "advice" on what she should do about it. But she was relentless. She knew that she had to bring me into this world, despite the world not wanting me here. She felt something telling her that I needed to be here. Nothing made her more sure of that than the day I was born. And every day after, she remained so glad that she didn't let the naysayers affect her decision. She was faithful to let me know, too, that I had purpose on this earth, because if my dad had had his way, I likely wouldn't be here.

My mom acted as both of my parents and she was literally a boss while raising my sister and I; she still is. She did everything she had to do to take care of us and make sure we didn't go without. My mom didn't have it easy growing up either. She was born to my grandmother while she was in college and unmarried. My great-grandmother and grandmother decided it would be best for my mom to be adopted so my grandmother could finish school. Luckily, my mom was born into a huge family with people that had the ability to take her in, so she was adopted by her great aunt and her husband; my Nana and late Papap. Nana already had 8 children, so my mom made the 9th (yes that's N I N E children); the 60's & 70's were something else. Nana and Papap were so selfless to take my mom in and raise her as if she was their own. She got so much love (and a whole lot of Jesus) being raised by them. But she was unwanted by her birth parents. My mom had voids that no one told her about either.

Throughout her childhood, my mom lived in a few different homes: Nana and Papap's, another great aunt, and she even tried to live with her birth mother at some point to try and build a relationship with her. The inconsistencies, voids, and feelings of being undesired caught up with her as a late teen. She started getting into trouble, acting out, and running away. But honestly, she was just a kid who was missing something that she wasn't even aware wasn't there. My mom got pregnant with my sister and had her at 18 years old, and then she got pregnant with me and had me at 20 years old. She repeated the same cycle as her mother.

I think our births kicked my mom straight. Like all of her crazy stopped after we were born, and she was determined to be the best mother she could be. I think she was determined to give us the kind of love that she never felt like she had. And she did. I will never be able to repay her for that. I am so loved by my mother.

We lived in Wheeling, WV, and my mom went to community college to get her associates degree while we were still young. I can remember, when I was 3-4 years old, going to class with her and sitting on the floor by her desk; that's how determined she was to create a better future for us. She got her degree and realized that Wheeling was not the best place to raise her kids, so she moved us to Montgomery County, MD, where we were able to get an amazing education. My mom spent her life giving everything she could to make sure we had everything we needed. She sacrificed, went without, and overcompensated for the fathers that weren't in either of our lives. She was and is an amazing, God-fearing, loving mother, and yet, somehow, I still had a void. It's unfortunate that a missing parents' deficiencies could overshadow a present parents' love. Her overcompensation could never make up for the things that he was supposed to provide as the father. When I think of God and how the Holy Trinity, the Father, the Son, and the Spirit, and how they all have distinguished roles, I can't imagine not having one of them. I wouldn't be here if not for the Father. I couldn't see salvation if not for the Son. And I couldn't keep my salvation if not for the Holy Spirit. I need all three Persons. You couldn't remove one part of the Trinity and expect me to be okay.

The father is supposed to be the first person to show his daughter how a man is supposed to love her; he's supposed to be a stable person in her life, and he's supposed to be a provider, amongst many other things. I had these things from my mom, of course, but my dad was in and out of my life for a while and then just consistently out. Any girl growing up without a dad can probably attest to the fact that no matter how much love you have coming from other family and friends, it never feels like enough to make up for the love that's supposed to be coming from your father. So, as horrible as it sounds because my mom loved me so well, I never felt fully loved. If I journey back to my 13-year-old mind, I remember thoughts of my mom's love and how I felt like it was "mandatory". As a child, the mandatory love didn't feel as special (sorry mom). But, when I would think of my dad, his love felt like it was an option, and his choice was to not love me. That hurt more than the mandatory love could make up for.

But even God operates like this, right? He gives us free will so that we choose to acknowledge His love for us and then love Him back. He doesn't make loving Him mandatory. The difference is, He isn't dependent on our love. I know now that my mom's love was that unconditional, selfless love that I get from my Heavenly Father, but back then it felt like it was just mandatory; she wasn't allowed to not love me, so it almost didn't count. My dad's love, however, was his choice and he made a choice that I wasn't enough for him. He made me feel like I wasn't good enough to love so, in my mind, I wasn't loved.

There was a brief portion of my childhood that I

remember feeling loved by a father-like figure. While we were living in Wheeling, WV, my mom lived with Nana and Papap for a while. Nana's youngest son was a few years older than my mom, so he was living in my grandparent's house with my mom, my sister, and I. I think Uncle Phillip was the first man that loved me. After I was born, he was attached to me. My mom told me stories of how'd he take care of me, consistently hold me (even when I didn't need to be held), love on me, and spend intentional quality time with me. During that 1-2 years that we lived with Uncle Phillip, an attachment formed, so much so that he would always tell the family that I was his favorite niece; and with 8 brothers and sisters, there were a lot of nieces and nephews. And it's pretty easy to conclude that he was my favorite uncle. Thinking back to after we moved away from West Virginia, I can remember times when I was so frustrated with my mom and my first thoughts would be "I wish I could go live with Uncle Phillip." His love for me was so ingrained into my heart that I didn't even know why I was attached, but he was the one I wanted to run to. It wasn't until my mom reminded me of how much he coddled me as a baby that it all started to make sense. He was my favorite because at my unconscious age, when I had dependency, he poured consistent love into me and showed me that I mattered. And even as a baby with an undeveloped brain, I carried that with me into early adolescence. I knew, firmly, that I was loved by him. Thank you, Uncle Phillip.

But we moved away from Uncle Phillip and Wheeling, and the distance was strong enough to negate the confirmation that I was loved. I guess our hearts require consistent refilling. When people pour out their love, your body acknowledges that. But if or when it goes away, you're right back to feeling unloved.

I knew God growing up. I was raised in the church from the moment I was born. My Nana was the Pastor of a church in Wheeling called "Emmanuel Tabernacle Baptist Church, Apostolic Faith" – yes, that was the entire name of the church. I was baptized at the age of 5, and I was saved at the age of 16; I knew that I was "loved" by God. But, my definition of love wasn't shaped by the sacrificial or unconditional denotation that God gave us. So, what did being loved by God really even mean when I was young?

Picture a cup with a small hole on the side. Its entire life's purpose is to be filled with something. When nothing is in it it's yearning to be poured into, and when it's poured into it holds the substance for a while.

However, at some point, it runs out when the water fills up to where the hole is. This was my heart. No father around and I felt unlovable and unloved. As I became an adult, I got a better understanding of how God can and will fill that void, but as a young, impressionable girl, I didn't understand that. I was so desperate for love, even while my mind wasn't able to build a concrete concept of what love was. My dad tried to show up at random times in my life, but he always failed me. As I got older, I became more aware of what he wasn't doing and started becoming confused as to why he couldn't be consistent or keep his promises.

I was a young girl with a void but had no idea that the void was present until I became an adult. I spent my entire adolescence unaware of my lack. We're born with this dependency to be loved. God's love is our overwhelming supply, but as a child, our parent's love is our tangible reality of God's love. When this dependency isn't filled, we have a void. But what 12-year-old knows and understands that? All a pre-teen feels is that something is missing in their life. And how could I have known it was love that was missing? I have family that loves me, and I'm going to church every Sunday and being told that God loves me. But there is something or, better yet, someone who is physically missing. So, I homed in on my father's presence as the thing that was missing. I never even consider that it wasn't necessarily his presence that my heart is yearning for; it was the love that he was supposed to give. And because life is so fair and God has a sense of humor, I'm experiencing this void at the same time I'm hitting puberty, and I'm a girl. Best. Deal. Ever. With frustration growing because something is missing, I filled my void with anger towards my father for simply failing to be around.

Enter anger. To be honest, anger didn't come into the void irate It came into my void as peace; as something I could hold on to because it filled what was missing, and I could control it. Anger filled my void, so I wasn't in lack anymore. I was able to be me, or a version of me that I believed to be real. I could finally stop worrying about what's missing and focus on something that I have. A void is just an empty space; it doesn't care what substance fills it, as long as it's filled. I didn't feel like something was missing anymore. I was content.

It wasn't fair, though. I was just a kid, and I had no idea what was happening. I was being consumed by this principality called anger, which was bred by a void; that void was created by a dependency someone didn't fulfill. I didn't choose this. I didn't want this either. And sadly, no one around me could do anything about it, because these types of things aren't noticed, understood, or discussed. It wasn't fair.

When I say anger entered my puzzle, I don't mean casually. I'm not talking about a typical teenage attitude. I was an angry child. If you didn't know me before I was 18, you likely wouldn't believe that about me, because I'm such a bubbly, happy person now. But in my early teens, and even in childhood, I was angry at everyone and no one at the same time. By the time I turned 14, it had gotten so bad that it was recommended I attend anger management courses. My first year of high school, I entered in as a problem child. Not because I was one but because I unknowingly allowed something that I knew nothing about to fill me up where love should have been. In high school, the manifestation of anger was very real. I got really good grades, I was active in extracurricular activities, but I was unhappy, and it showed. When I turned 17, the overwhelming sense of something being wrong, but not knowing what it is, came to a head. I took my anger out on my mom and ran away for 2 days. I chalked it up to "being misunderstood" and "not feeling heard." Now, don't get me wrong, those are very real feelings, and I was definitely feeling that at the time, but it wasn't my mom that was misunderstanding me. It was me that was misunderstanding me.

My lack of understanding got the best of me. I didn't know who I was or what I was doing (as most teenagers don't). On top of that, I allowed something that was never supposed to be a part of my identity creep in and define me. I allowed it to consume and control me and, worst of all, I allowed it to hurt the one person that I knew loved me.

> That's how powerful voids are. You feel like you need something so you run to anything, because that's human nature. You're in need of something, so you go looking for it. And it's not a mistake. God didn't mess up when He made us like this. This was intentional for His will.

That's how powerful voids are. You feel like you need something so you run to anything, because that's human nature. You're in need of something, so you go looking for it. And it's not a mistake. God didn't mess up when He made us like this. This was intentional for His will. He made us like this so that we would seek Him, so that we'd never stop chasing after Him. As humans, born into sin and ignorance, we don't always catch on to the fact that it's God that we're dependent on, so we chase anything for a fix to fill the void. But then, even when we get a fix of something, we remain thirsty because we choose to fill our dependencies with things that run out instead of God's love, which is a well that never runs dry. It's like drinking saltwater when you haven't hydrated in days. When lack of fulfillment of a dependency happens and the void opens up, your war begins. And that's what happened to me. I was at war. Things that I knew nothing about were rushing into my life, attempting to fill that void. Demons saw an empty space in a vulnerable girl and flocked at the oppurtunity to insert unwarranted and damaging pieces into her puzzle. If you don't realize you're at war, you'll continue to feed the very thing you should be fighting. And this, my friends, is where my counterfeit picture began.

Proverbs 22:6 says "Train up a child in the way that he should go and when is old, he will not depart from it" (NIV). We often quote this scripture in hopes of helping people understand the importance of instilling the right values and lessons into their children while they're young. If you grew up in a family like mine, you probably heard it as a means to justify making a 5-year-old stay awake in church or whooping a child (just kidding, but seriously). In his sermon All Strings Attached, Pastor Mike Todd presented the question "what if you were trained wrong?" We often review the scripture in light of positive training, but he's presenting a potential reality that we might unknowingly be taught incorrectly with habits that parents don't even pay attention to. The scripture is true: what we're taught while we're young sticks with us. Parents may focus on making sure we have the correct morals and values, but what about love? Are we accurately taught what it really is? Is it assumed that it's learned through our parent's actions? If so, what if our parent's actions aren't displaying love properly? Are we taught how dependent we are on the right kind of love? Are we taught how to love ourselves...correctly?

The example of love that I received from an absent parent was wishy washy, conditional, and unstable; it wasn't real love. And while I was shown real love from my mom and family, I was still trained wrong. With a stable love from my mom and an unstable love from my dad, I learned that love from a parent was optional. You could decide to love your child or not to. Honestly, this isn't an abnormal thing anymore. It's pretty typical to see a parent decide not to stick around. What's unfortunate is that the parent who doesn't stick around teaches the child more about love than the parent who stays. The parent who stays is simply doing what they're supposed to. The parent who leaves or never intends to be in a child's life shows the child that their presence in this world isn't enough to make them do what they're supposed to do. That absence teaches that love is conditional, sporadic, isolating, and hopeless. And that's how a child will begin to love people, God, and themselves.

I was trained wrong.

Counterfeit

Coun·ter·feit
/ˈkoun(t)ərˌfit/

adjective

1. Made in exact imitation of something valuable or important with the intention to deceive or defraud.

The empty space that I had left a massive opportunity for counterfeit pieces. Instead of being full of love and truth, I was an open door waiting to be filled with lies. Anger was the first counterfeit piece to enter my empty space. Next, came the worst pieces: difference, insecurity, shame, unworthiness, and anxiety. These pieces gave my picture definition, and it's what produced my mirage.

These counterfeit pieces, as a collection, did the most damage. Yeah, the void was the doorway but once these things entered, they directed the story of my life.

They worked together harmoniously to create the augmented reality of who I was, but was never supposed to be, for 25 years. The manifestation of the void that produced anger and an improper concept of love shaped the image of teenage and young adult Tyeisha, and she was DAMAGED. The void that my dad created made me feel like I wasn't good enough. He disqualified me before my race even began. And then, difference, insecurity, shame, unworthiness, and anxiety came along to solidify that I wasn't fit to be who God made me to be. So, what's the point of trying?

DIFFERENCE

It's so interesting how the generation after millennials, gen z, is defined by their difference and uniqueness. I grew up in the late 90's and early 2000's, and back then, being different wasn't something to be proud of. I was mocked and ridiculed for my difference, so standing out was not something I aimed for. I think that context is important in understanding how my feelings about difference fed the war that I was fighting as I was being molded into the person I wasn't supposed to become.

I was different, and I thought that was a curse. Sort of like those characters in the Bible with noticeable physical limitations that help explain how evident it was that they weren't supposed to be chosen, and it helped explain the magnitude of their victory. You wouldn't expect them to be, but somehow they were still chosen. I felt like Moses, who stuttered, or David, who was small in comparison to other people, let alone a giant. I didn't have a physical limitation, but that's how big my difference felt. It felt like something that was holding me back from who I so desperately wanted to be, and I felt like everyone could see it.

If I could give advice to anyone currently facing the idea that difference is a bad thing, I would tell them to embrace what God put in you. What He put in you, He wants to get back out of you and use it to His glory. Your God-created uniqueness is what God gives you to magnify the weight of your testimony. And whatever your uniqueness is, age has no bearing on when you can activate it. Embrace it now. You don't have to wait until you become an adult to find your place in this world. You have a place in His kingdom right now, and you can secure it by being happy about the way God made you and not letting anyone

> ❝ Your God-created uniqueness is what God gives you to magnify the weight of your testimony. ❞

make you feel like you're not a masterpiece.

But at that time, I wanted so badly to be the normal girl. The one that just fit in with no effort, like my friends. I wanted to fit a mold, not knowing or understanding that the way that God designed me objected conformity. So, God just let me be different, not able to fit in, no concept of why, and angry at the world with no concept of love for myself. Cool.

I was awkward, confused, lost, unloved, and I simply didn't want to be that girl. The voices in my head told me that I didn't fit in, and it made me run to conformity. Those voices screamed so loud that I swear people at school could hear them. So, in effort to prove them wrong, I sought out ways to fit in. Fitting in, in this picture, looked like me shoving puzzle pieces in the wrong places just so I'd have some semblance of normalcy, regardless of if it was the picture intended or not.

Around the age of 13, I found a crowd of people who accepted me. It didn't matter if I accepted their lack of values or who they were, they accepted me, and that was enough. It was so easy to inject myself in their group because they lived in my neighborhood, and we went to the same school, and they didn't care if you were "weird" or not; they just accepted you. But predictably, these were the bad kids in the neighborhood. Through the fights, theft, and all around ratchetness that this group was about, I knew I was nothing like them, but they accepted me and that's all that mattered. I didn't necessarily participate in their shenanigans, but I hung around them all of the time and they called me a friend. This was so important to me – feeling accepted in spite of. I realize now that being accepted was so important to me because I didn't accept myself; I didn't love myself. And how could I? I didn't know the first thing about it.

INSECURITY

The girls in this group introduced to me the lie that the love I needed could come from a guy. Let me explain here that I was sheltered. My mom did a great job at shielding my sister and I from a lot of things. I was hanging with a rough crowd but not participating in any of the crazy things that they were doing at the age of 13. So, needless to say, I wasn't hip to the idea that girls my age were seeking love from guys and actually getting [false] love back. They looked so happy and so fulfilled, and I couldn't figure out for the life of me why I wasn't doing the same.

Through these girls, I was introduced to guys who preyed on young girls like me. My difference created severe insecurity, which - let's be real - is way too common for teenagers in general, let alone female teenagers who grew up in a single parent home. This crippling identity crisis made me a prime candidate to be taken advantage of by any guy that paid attention to me and made it extremely hard to resist one of the first guys who ever noticed me. I was never supposed to be noticed because I was so different. At that time, I thought I was too dark-skinned and ugly as well. I stuck out like a sore thumb in the worst ways, so how in the world could this guy notice and choose to pursue me out of all the normal people around me. I was so overwhelmed at the thought that someone was paying attention to me. It didn't matter that he was 19 and, yes, I was still 13.

The idea that I wasn't damaged goods that no one wanted hit me so fast and so hard. Within days of realizing that there was someone who noticed me, I found myself coming out of my shell to make sure I was front and center whenever he was around. I paid more attention to my hair and my clothes had to compliment what

little bit of "assets" I had to make sure I was noticeable. Reflecting on this as an adult makes my stomach
turn. I was 13 years old, trying to make sure a 19-year-
old guy could see my barely developed body through
my clothes, because that's how I was taught I could
fill my voids. I was a baby trying to prostitute myself
for any version of love that I could get. Not one of the
girls that I was hanging with saw any flaw in this; they
encouraged it. They did everything they could to make
sure we had opportunities to see each other. They were
my biggest supporters when it came to finding false
love that was really just lust and would lead to more
counterfeit pieces in my life. It's clear that they had
voids too. Damaged people damage people.

I could go into further detail about all of our in-
teractions that led up to this ultimate event that would
shape the next 15 years of my life, but I'll spare you
the cliché. I was insecure, I didn't love myself, I saw
my difference as a curse, and he made me feel like it
wasn't. It's hard to say even now, but honestly he made
it easy to give myself to him. At 13, I lost my virginity
to a legal adult. But before you start to pity me and
view him as predatorial, consider this: he was likely
suffering with his own unacknowledged voids and

identity crisis. So, while he may have been older, is it right to hold him more accountable than me? After all, neither of us were operating with the right pieces, and I know what it's like to be an adult with unaddressed voids.

I'm not one to regret many things. To me, you win or learn; there's no losing. But losing my virginity at such a young age bred so much damage in my picture. It's the one thing that Id change if I could go back. Not so much because of the whole sexual immorality piece but because I was 13. I had just hit puberty, and I had welcomed the damage and despair that would come from my body being used like a toy. I welcomed the mind games that came from my belief that this would lead to the love I desperately desired. I was a baby in a warzone and I essentially sat on the battlelines, defenseless by giving my unloved self to someone who had no intention of loving me. Hello insecurity!

As you would imagine, after the guy got what he wanted, he bolted. There was nothing left to stick around for, leaving me with that insecurity and confirmation that I wasn't loved and no one wanted to love me. He left me seeking more of that temporary fix. Even though it was short lived and left me damaged, he did make me forget my difference for a while. And, in the moment, I felt wanted; I felt loved. My sexuality was shaped here by my insecurity. I made a conscious decision to pursue men for the sake of finding someone that would be a permanent fix to dispelling my difference; if sex was necessary to do so, I was willing. I also started only looking at older guys. I don't think that I was actually attracted to boys my age at any point after that.

SHAME/UNWORTHINESS

In the summer of 2005, I was 14 years old and I was babysitting my mom's co-worker's daughter for the entire summer. She lived in a neighborhood just across the street from mine, so I'd walk back and forth every day for my summer job. One day, as I was walking home, a black car with all black windows stopped me in my neighborhood. I was alarmed at first until he rolled down the window and I saw it was a semi-cute guy trying to talk to me. My guard immediately went down.

We'll call this guy Joe for the sake of anonymity. Joe told me that he had been watching me for days now when I would come home but he hadn't had a chance to stop and say anything yet. He told me I was cute, that I looked like I had my head on straight, and that I deserved a man like him in my life. He also told me he was a rapper 😄. All the things my 14-year-old, damaged self did not need to hear. Now, you're probably thinking "he's driving, how old is this guy?!" I was too. I asked, and he told me that he was 18, which, I'm going to be honest, he looked nothing like. If any of you could see a picture of this guy, you'd likely put him between 27-32. But the naïve, 14-year-old, desperate-for-attention Tyeisha accepted him being 18 gladly (as if 18 years old wasn't too old). I later learned that he was in fact about 25 years old from a family member who he had also tried to talk to. Nonetheless, Joe got my number and man was I excited. Another guy noticed me, and this one could drive. I was stepping up my game; I didn't even have to do anything to pull this one.

I think Joe and I only texted/talked on the phone for about one month total. Most of the time was spent flirting. I don't remember the extent of our conversations, but I do remember that it was a back and forth cat and mouse game. We never got to specifics of who we were, what we wanted out of life, or talking about dating. I didn't think this was abnormal though, I loved having someone in my phone showing me attention and flirting with me. For context, though I had been sexually active, flirting for me at 14 years old was as naïve and innocent as you might think. He'd tell me to send a picture, I would send a selfie of just my face, he'd compliment me, and I'd blush. We probably talked about kissing or simply hanging out but nothing more extensive than that.

After weeks of the cat and mouse game, he started to get anxious about hanging with me. My mom was strict, and I was sheltered, so I couldn't just casually hang out with someone whenever I wanted, especially a boy. So, I had to figure out how to hang with him. By the end of the summer, I was working at an ice cream shop that was about 5 minutes away from my house. I'd get off around 7 or 8pm, and usually my mom or sister would come pick me up. One night, Joe and I decided that we'd finally try to hang for a while, and he would be the one to take me home. I made up some story to my mom about my best friend taking me home so she didn't have to come get me. I was so excited that a guy was picking me up from work. It made me feel so adultish. I knew we didn't have much time together but, we had waited so long, it was enough to just sit with him in his car for a few moments.

He picked me up from work that night with the direction to take me home. He had other intentions though. He decided we could hang at his apartment instead, so he started heading that way. It was the exact opposite direction from my house, so we had a prompt conversation about what was going on. I told him that I live 5 minutes away and that my mom was expecting me home asap; I would be in so much trouble if I didn't come home right away. As my concern grew, I think he realized going to his house wasn't really an option, so he stopped along the way at a park and got out the car. My concern turned to worry because now I'm 10 minutes away from my house by car, and he seems angry. At this point, I am adamantly asking him to take me home as my mom starts texting me asking where I'm at. His demeanor was pretty nonchalant about my plight as he continued to walk further into the park and sit on a picnic table.

The phone calls from my mom began, and I wasn't picking up because I had no idea what my story was going to be. I got out of the car and begged him to please take me home; I was petrified of my mom and what she'd do if I didn't answer my phone or come home shortly. My emotions were welling up at this point, and it was clear that I was flustered and scared. All the while, he remained unphased. His rebuttal to why he would not take me home when I begged him was that I led him to believe that we were going to have sex, and he wasn't taking me home until we did. My naïve self is flabbergasted at this point. We hadn't discussed sex one time. It actually made me think that he was so different because he wasn't asking for that. I realize, now that I'm an adult, a lot of men (and some women) will take simple flirting as an invitation for sex. So, apparently, I had summoned him for sex and wasn't pulling through on my end. I did not want to have sex with him.

Tears were now supporting my plea to be taken home because I was scared out of my mind, and I had no other way to get home. But with tears streaming down my face in fear of him and my mom, Joe looked at me and told me that tears didn't phase him. He told me that I'm either having sex with him or I'm walking home. Although my mom would have come in a heartbeat, I simply couldn't let her know what I had gotten myself into; after all, this was my fault. I lied to her

47

and decided to get into a car with a guy I didn't know. I was more afraid of her reaction to my failure than anything else at that point. So, I made what I thought was my decision to have sex with him, in a park, just so I could be taken home. I would later understand that that was rape.

When he was finished, I remember him saying "Now that wasn't so hard was it? That's all I wanted." At the time, I never considered it to be rape because I agreed for the sake of my safe return home. And I was returned home physically safe but mentally and emotionally destroyed. I remember how broken I was that night, but I couldn't show it or tell anyone what was going on. I remember thinking "This was on me! I made the decision to go with him and I consented to what he wanted so I could come home." While I didn't think he was right for forcing me to do it, I blamed myself 100% for the events of that night. I didn't know until I was 28 that I was actually a victim that night.

Let me pause here for a moment and acknowledge the volume of young women who endure this. As normal as single parent households are today, the sexual assault of young women is just as common, unacknowledged sexual assault even more so. A lot of times, young women are made to feel like it was their fault: they enticed him or they consent out of fear or out of coercion. It's still rape, and I want to let you know that it's never your fault. Men (and women for that matter) have to accept that no means no, and after she (or he) has said no, what happens after that is rape.

But I blamed myself and I carried that with me at the forefront of my mind throughout my teenage years, and then buried it deep inside me in adulthood. So much so that I didn't even remember it happened to me until I started to be disassembled.

Fast forward to my young adult years, the danger of the culmination of all of these things was the façade they bred. From that moment on, I'd never be the same. Now, on top of the void, anger, lack of love for myself, difference, and insecurity, my friends unworthiness and shame came along for the ride. I wasn't burdened with unworthiness and shame; they were an escape. If I wasn't worth anything, suddenly the dependency to love or be loved doesn't seem as strong. And if I'm not dependent on being loved anymore there's no reason to be angry [exit anger]. Giving my purity away and then being sexually assaulted drove me to escape to a world of false love where my void was filled, but in a hologram sort of way. Love was there, but not really.

I spent years trying to work out the kinks that jamming these pieces into the puzzle created. They didn't feel like they belonged, but it's all I really knew, so maybe they did. My mind and body were working double time simply growing but also trying to reconcile what had happened to me and trying to determine who I was, so maybe triple time. It was draining. I developed a lot of coping mechanisms during this time; one of which was talking to boys on the internet. And while this might seem normal today, it was not so normal back in the early 2000's. I joined chat rooms and found boys on AOL instant messenger to chat with and dote on me. I even "dated" a few of them. I never met them in person, but I was "in love" and committed to them (as in love and committed as a 15-year-old girl could be). They helped me feel worthy and like I deserved something that shame was telling me I didn't. They helped me escape from the reality of my shame and indulge myself in a virtual reality of love. This translated a lot in my early 20's, when online dating became popular and normal. I found pleasure in losing myself in complete strangers that only knew the pieces of me that I would allow them to. They weren't around to see the whole picture, so I could be anyone I wanted to be.

At this point, it was clear that I had lost all sense of self, or never had it for that matter. I was getting older and realizing that someone worth loving was supposed to be forming, and I was supposed to love her. I realized that I should love myself at this point and I didn't. Not just because I didn't know the first thing about love, but because there was nothing attractive about me to me. All I saw was desperation, and she was ugly. I needed to find something worth holding on to again. I needed to find something that would help me reconcile what had happened in my life up to this point, and it needed to be something I could find direction in to move forward. I did not like what I saw when I looked in the mirror, but I was determined to change that. God gave me that drive, so I ran to Him.

I gave my life to Christ at the age of 16, a few years after losing my virginity and being assaulted. This is where my quest to feel redemption began, but it wouldn't be until 27 that I would actually feel like I received it. The thing I learned about God is that He never stops pursuing His children. He never throws in the towel or thinks that we're past the point of redemption. I didn't know it at the time, but my sin wasn't strong enough to stop the calling on my life. There's more grace in God than there is sin in me.

God pursued me. That's the reason I stand strong

There's more grace in God than there is sin in me.

today. And that consistent pursuit is what led me to give my life to Him. I remember thinking during the altar call that I need to "get my life together" before I give it to Him. I had sinned so much and being violated made me feel like my life wasn't good enough to be given to a Savior. I felt like there were things that I needed to change in my life before committing to "be good" the rest of my life. And this is how a lot of people feel when they're coming to Christ. They feel like they have to change their ways or that there's work they have to do within themselves before accepting Jesus in their lives. If no one has ever told you, let me be the first: this is a lie. It's one of the greatest tools of deception that Satan will use to deter you from committing to God. After thinking that, I remember God telling me that I didn't need to fix anything before giving my life to Him and that He would take care of the "fixing" once I declare that He died on a cross to save me from my sin. After all, His name is "Savior", right? So, I did, and it was the best decision that I ever made.

The next 10 years of my life were spent seeking redemption. While God offered forgiveness to me immediately, I didn't give it to myself until I started breaking. And those 10 years were brutal. People assume that once you give your life to Christ, things get easier: NOT TRUE. I love God, I promise, but to be blunt, He didn't make my life any easier because I chose Him, and I didn't realize that's what I was signing up for. I thought I was getting an easier life, but what I got was a friend that would come alongside me to heal me and be with me along the way.

After I gave my life to Christ, God started to reveal to me how the difference that I felt for so long was His calling. This uniqueness was a gift and not a curse; my sin didn't cancel it [exit difference]. But it loomed over me like a curse for so long, and continued to, even after I found out it wasn't. Now that I know God intentionally made me different or unique to fulfill a calling that He has for me on this earth, I have to figure out how to be worth it. Now, I'm battling a battle within a battle. My sin didn't stop. If anything, it was just magnified because now I'm "saved," and I'm not supposed to sin. My self-loathing wasn't gone, and I hadn't figured out how to love myself. Nothing had really changed besides the fact that I now know that God made me for a reason. And now, every wrong thing I do is pulling me further and further away from that calling. My thinking at the time was that I was ruining my chances for God to keep loving me. Lies. I had so much shame for who I was and what I was doing. No parts of me thought I could still be used by God after all of my mistakes. More lies. *I'm literally nothing and so unworthy of even being looked at by God. I'm not good enough and never will be* – the worst lie of them all.

These are the feelings that I carried for 10 years: I'm not good enough, not worthy of God's calling, and not sure what to do with my life. I've continued to mess up God's plan for me, so what's my purpose now? After countless attempts to feel like I had been redeemed and feel "worthy" of God's purpose for my life, I gave up on the idea that I could use the uniqueness that God gave me for His good and set out to use it for worldly good. Giving up the idea of being a spiritual instrument, I set out to break stereotypical barriers and become well educated, successful, financially stable, and a mentor. And I did. But one thing that I learned about God is that God's plan always included my failures. And I now know that there's nothing that I could do to stop His plan or damage the gift that He intended to use. I'm not that powerful. So, while worldly success is all well and good, it wasn't good enough for what God wanted for me, and He didn't give up on me like

I gave up on myself. In all of my worldly success, that feeling that something was missing always stuck around. That void didn't go away. And although I was trying to feed it with growth and worldly success, I couldn't shake the empty feeling. It didn't matter how many positive things were happening in my life, I wasn't where God wanted me to be, and I didn't believe in His undying love for me, so I still wasn't enough. No matter what, I just was not enough.

> **God's plan always included my failures.**

ANXIETY

Anxiety is like a disease. It just shows up. No one asks for it or invites it in. Like most man-made diseases that are on a rise these days, it usually comes by way of habits built up over time. It comes by way of innate behaviors that are not abnormal or unusual, but the repetition of the unhealthy behavior builds a repertoire of habits that create diseases like anxiety. Most of them also creep up on you, and then, out of nowhere, overtake your life and everything you've worked to build. Difference, insecurity, shame, and unworthiness bred this disease in my mind.

I didn't know what anxiety truly was until I was an adult. When I was a child, anxiety was my friend. Those voices from before that were consistently screaming at me about my difference, that was anxiety. It spoke good and bad but, no matter what, it spoke what I believed to be truth. And no matter what, it was there for me. It was a friend to talk to when no one else would listen or understand, when I didn't have a voice and I was the most insignificant person in the world. It was my friend and I thought it loved me because it was there. Not that it did any good for me, but it was present. At this point, I judged love by presence.

The voice in my head was all that I had when I was faced with insecurity about being so different. I could talk to that voice and be open and honest about everything and, although I'd receive judgement back, at least I could express my true feelings. I could talk to this voice and tell this voice how out of place I felt, how awkward I felt, and how inadequate I felt. And the voice would talk back and encourage my self-doubt. It would feed my self-loathing and then tell me that there was nothing that could be done right now. That I'm young and there was nothing that I could change about myself to make me fit in, so I'd have to sit and wait until I got older and I could be who I wanted to be. I remember always thinking that I couldn't wait to be an adult, because then I would shine.

I was so deceived. I feel sorry for high school me as I look back, because I listened attentively and accepted what it said, but the voice lied and omitted things that I didn't realize until now. See, I DID NOT have to wait until I became an adult to find out that I belonged. I DID NOT have to change anything about myself to be adequate and I DID NOT need to be anything or anyone else to stop doubting myself. I needed to know God's love for me! I needed to understand His grace. But all the voice was doing was building a rapport with me so I'd trust it, which actually drove my isolation from others and led to the personification of the voice as anxiety. See, the voice neglected to mention throughout all of the years that it listened to my problems and gave me "advice" on how to handle it in that moment that it had two sides, like sour patch kids. Only, with this voice, first it's sweet and then sour. As I became an adult, it would turn into crippling anxiety and start to destroy me.

Let me again remind you that I was saved by this time. I was in church every Sunday, at every Church event, and had a praying mother and family. This is important because some people might look at these struggles and think that I didn't know Jesus or that I didn't have the correct guidance in life. And some people look at those who do have Jesus in their life and think that they should just be okay because of that fact, not so. Mental illness is real. But like I mentioned, this disease, it comes by way of normal day to day activities: feeling insecure, not having a voice, and being alone. It's birthed by these "normal" things that teens go through, and it's left to grow and thrive when you don't truly understand Jesus' love and grace. Knowing His love and grace could have taught me I don't need a single soul to understand my strife because my Father does, and He's made plans for it. It could have taught me that that my difference was masterminded before the world was even thought of.

It also grows when you take your eyes off Jesus. When you lose focus of your Father, you fall like Peter did while walking on water. He took his eyes off Jesus for a moment and lost his balance, which made him vulnerable. Satan feeds on that vulnerability; it's an open playing field for him to plant thoughts of unworthiness, loneliness, destruction, and suicide. But I didn't know this, and I was misguided by my "friend" to think that this was normal and would be conquered when I became an adult.

When I left for college is when this voice began showing itself as a disease. It finally started showing symptoms of its horrid nature. The symptoms varied, but the ones that showed themselves loud and strong were control issues, overcompensation, fear and, of course, depression. Anxiety and fear created a desperate need for me to be in control. My mom always described my control issues as me being an "independent young lady"; that was the nicest way it could have been categorized. But really, I needed to be in control, and if I wasn't, anxiety took over. So, in essence, anxiety led to control issues, which led to more anxiety.

I discovered that I had control issues during the breaking process. I had no idea before then. I fly pretty often for work and, like a lot of people, I would always get nervous. To be honest, these used to be the times that I talked to God the most, because I was praying consistently for 1-3 hours at a time while on planes. For years, my calming method was to put in headphones and watch a movie. That way, I wouldn't really feel like I was on a plane. It acted as an escape from realizing where I was. One day, in really bad turbulence, I became overwhelmed with anxiety. I prayed and asked God why I'm so anxious about this when I know that He's protecting me and I know that He won't let anything happen to me, because He made me a promise of life that I still need to walk in. So why am I so scared? Car accidents are far more frequent than plane accidents. In asking this, God helped me dissect what was at the foundation of my fear and showed me that I'm not afraid of driving a car because I'm behind the wheel. On a plane, I have to sit back and trust God with what I don't understand, and my life is literally on the line. I didn't trust Him, not really. I wanted to be in control of the plane. I needed to know exactly how the plane worked to give me assurance that it wouldn't go down. The fact that I didn't know how it worked and I didn't have control over my life in those moments on airplanes made me anxious. This is when I discovered my control issues. It's like I thought that in every other moment I had control over my life, except for when my feet weren't on the ground. This was pretty egregious thinking.

God used this to show me that I didn't trust Him with my life. And it was true; I didn't. Not actually trusting Him with my life only furthered the anxiety I had. Now that I'm on the other side, I can see clearly what He was trying to get me to see, and I can now say that my life is confidently in His hands on and off planes. I don't fear losing control in any situation anymore because, the reality is, I never had it. The best way for me to gain control was for me to lose it and trust the person Who has it.

But anxiety told me that I couldn't trust anyone and that, in order for me to protect myself, I needed to be in control. Anxiety started to manifest itself through all of these symptoms, but the worse part was that I didn't even have my "friend" anymore. It morphed into my enemy, because it was destroying me. So now, I was dealing with even more

The best way for me to gain control was for me to lose it and trust the person who has it.

counterfeit pieces, trying to figure them all out, and I was doing it alone.

There is a documentary called *What the Health* on Netflix and one of the things that I learned from watching it is that many diseases that exist today are man-made diseases: heart disease, Alzheimer's disease, cancer, etc. And what the documentary explains is that these diseases are birthed by the food we eat and the animals we consume. The way that some of the animals we eat are fed and raised create diseased environments in their bodies, and we then eat them. And over time, a normal habit like eating meat could be causing your demise. I think anxiety is like that. We might not even be drinking directly from the fountain of insecurity, but we're getting it second hand because this voice that's supposed to be our peace is telling us that we're not good enough right now, but we might be later. So, we unknowingly let insecurity, shame, and unworthiness in over and over and over, until somewhere along the line you develop this disease called anxiety. And by this time, we're attached to it, because it started as our friend. It might not be behaving like a friend right now, but we can't neglect the fact that it was once a friend. Just like when I was battling my fear of flying and God made me look beneath the symptom to uncover the actual issue, we have to start addressing the issues beneath anxiety in people.

So many people, both young and old, battle with this disease: anxiety. I believe that if we look at it for what it is, an old friend that's just been around for way too long, it becomes easier for us to grasp the severity of its effects and control on us. And I believe that once we grasp how severe it's affects are, we can start to peel back the layers of what's beneath the surface of it and understand the root problem. We originally invited it in; we're not born with it. Whether consciously or subconsciously, we allowed it in, which means we have the power to tell it to go. It may not feel like it because it's like letting a piece of yourself go, and who knows how to do that!?

The longer we allow it to linger undiagnosed, it festers and makes a home for itself. This is why we think it can't be defeated and why we think we can't overpower it. This is also why sometimes our efforts to drown ourselves in God and His word seem pointless after we're living with this disease. We're stacking hope and prosperity on top of the disease, but we're not actually curing or releasing it. This is what's called the "trick of the enemy." I heard it all of my life in my family and in church. It's such a cliché, but we have to understand how he works. He tricks us. He tries to make us think that we don't have power over those things, but we do. God gave it to us: "We demolish arguments and every pretension that sets itself up against the knowledge of God, and we take captive every thought to make it obedient to Christ" (2 Corinthians 10:5, NIV). No shame, no hurt, no anxiety, and no principality has more power than God has given us. But the enemy tricks us to believe that we are inferior to the obstacles set before us, taking the fight out of us before we can even start. So, even though you know God, you love Him, and you think that you trust Him, you're still in fear of everything, unable to let go of anything without knowing why.

SPACE

space
/spās/

noun

1. a continuous area or expanse which is free, available, or unoccupied

So, here I am with all of my counterfeit pieces, forming a picture through a struggle to find worth and living in consistent fear of everything and nothing for no reason at all. The misguidance and misunderstandings led to sinful and empty teenage and young adult years, even with my salvation intact. I was a warped image…and the sad part is that you'd never know. There were crumbled pieces, wrong colors, missing pieces, some lodged into places that they don't belong, and some that didn't belong at all. But still, it was a picture. And only the Manufacturer who knew what the image was supposed to be could see how wrong it was. The world accepted it. I was a 27-year-old young, black female who, by the world's standard, was successful with a career, financially stable, had a great family, wasn't married yet, had no kids, and had a little bit of God sprinkled on a few of my puzzle pieces. I could have gone the rest of my life with this façade and nothing would have appeared wrong. But when God has His hands on you, He doesn't want to just be a few of the pieces in your puzzle. He wants to be the glue that connects all the pieces together. He wants to be the foundation of who you are because, after all, we are His. So, if your picture is wrong, even after 27 years of making it, He'll tear it down and ask you to start over again.

No matter how great it looked like I was doing, I never felt complete, even after my salvation and quest for redemption. Even through all of the promotions and growth at work, pursuing my MBA and MTS, and chasing my dreams, none of it ever made me feel whole. This feeling sat with me through every mountain that I was on because that void was never filled by anything that God intended for it. So, it didn't matter what worldly success came my way. It always felt pointless because I wasn't fulfilled. I always knew deep inside that I wasn't where God would have wanted me to be. The world wasn't good enough for me. It was that same feeling that my mom had while carrying me; that I had purpose here, and that feeling ate at me. That same feeling that she had about me after my conception is the same feeling that wouldn't let me be okay with "just okay." I just knew that I had something to do. I didn't know what it was, but I knew it was something. And as long as I wasn't doing it, I felt empty. That empty feeling sat with me through everything. Even when I tried to fill it with more church, it never amounted to anything fruitful or long-lasting. As a result, I kept seeking worldly gain, because, although it was temporary, it brought prosperity on this earth. And if I couldn't have a full spirit, I at least wanted a full wallet.

But God had more in store; settling wasn't a part of His plan for me.

I take no credit for the events in my life that led me into an actual relationship with God. He chased me down. He did it all; it was not by my hands. Similar to Paul and his Damascus road experience, God abruptly told me to leave the church that I been a part of for 5+

years with no growth. I was headed one way and then God just abruptly redirected me somewhere that led to my purpose. This is where I saw my favorite scripture, Philippians 1:6, start becoming a reality. In late 2017, I joined Elevation Church in Charlotte, NC. It took one visit to convince me that it was where I needed to be. Pastor Steven Furtick is one of the most amazing communicators of our generation and a devout student of the Word of God. I don't know where I'd be without him and the community that God gave me at this church. By finding a new church home, I ended 2017 with new convictions about who I was, Who's I was, and what I needed to do to grow.

April 1st, 2018 (Easter Sunday), God sent His Spirit to reconnect with me and call me back home. He didn't just call me into a new season, He came down from heaven to give me a ride to make sure I made it there. He sent the people that I needed to build my strength and consistency, and He sent me reminders that I was still called, still anointed, and that I still had purpose. My entire life didn't change that day, but my hope did. Hope that I could find love for myself, be redeemed, and live a life worth what God gave me was restored that day. A few weeks after Easter Sunday,

God sent Pastor Mike Todd to Elevation Church and he preached a sermon called Marked. I'm sure this sermon spoke to a lot of people that day but, for me, it was as if God sent him to assure me that I was chosen and still worthy of my calling. This was the confirmation and guidance I needed. I experienced resurrection on Easter and the sermon was my personal Pentecost. After this, I was able to establish a sincere commitment to Him, and I began to pursue relationship with God with intention and purpose. Man, I felt like a new person. I felt God's presence in my life guiding me, and I started hearing Him speak to me about my future. I had hope. I started being more consistent in my relationship with Him than I had ever been in the past, and I was more determined than ever to get it right this time. That year, I recommitted my purity to God, started serving at my church, started tithing, joined an e-group, and started leading a high school girls e-group. I started my fight. I was reclaiming my life and pressing forward to be who God wanted me to be, and it felt like a new beginning had come. What I'd soon find out was that it wasn't a new beginning but an abrupt end that was on the horizon for me.

I spent most of 2018 in a blissful new relationship

with God in which I started owning the fact that there was a process I had to go through to enable this new creature that He made me into. I began studying His word more intently and sharing this new identity that I found in Christ with the world. My mantra for 2018 was "trust the process," or I'd often quote Pastor Steven's sermon titled "Let the Dirt Do Its Work," and gosh I did. Every joyous moment and every heartache were met with optimism and hope for what they would produce in me. I was committed to the process and excited about what was next. I can imagine that God was laughing at my optimism, because He knew what was to come. As I trusted the process, God was telling me that I hadn't even scratched the surface of the process yet. In order to truly go through the process, I needed more of Him in my life. I know what you're thinking: church, leading/attending groups, studying His Word, and building a relationship with God...how much *more* of Him is possible?

I ended 2018 so excited about continued growth in my relationship with God. I started believing again and allowing myself to have hope that I'm still worth God's best. So, I began to write down what I wanted for my life in 2019. As I did, God started to speak to me the life of Matthew 6:33. He told me that if I give Him me, He'll open the windows of Heaven and pour me out blessings that I won't have room enough to receive, so I shouldn't seek the things that I wanted but rather Him so that He could give me everything I need. In other words, He wasn't telling me that I needed more of Him, He was telling me that He needed more of me.

Giving more of me didn't look like drowning myself in the things of God. It looked like me stopping everything that I was doing *for Him* so that I could be *with Him*. It looked like never-ending communion.

Let me take another moment here to speak to anyone that may feel like they're in this place, the place of trying to commit to God whole-heartedly while going to church, reading your Bible, and searching for Him, but He still seems so far. My plea to you is to never stop. It may be years of the same cycle in pursuit of Him—don't stop. You may feel like it's hopeless and a waste of time—don't stop. I've learned that our Heavenly Father chases us harder than we chase Him. And because He's in pursuit of you, you will connect; that's a given. But in order to connect, you can't be hidden away, and you can't lose hope. Hope is what fuels the journey. He's running to you at the same time you're running to Him. There will come a day that you arrive to find that He's been with you all along.

Space is an intentional emptiness that's created by removing things of uselessness for someone or something with greater purpose to fill it.

"Space" became my word and my focus as I walked into 2019. The difference between a void and space is this: voids are empty and unallocated because something was supposed to be there to fill it. Space is an intentional emptiness that's created by removing things of uselessness for someone or something with greater purpose to fill it. So, I set out on the year with the goal of being intentional about prioritizing my relationship with God, prioritizing time with Him. and clearing out a lot of the things in my life that were not like Him. God also took care of some of the house cleaning. He took care of removing a lot of things that I brought into my life because they were like Him: the things that I thought He would have me do. It's so funny to look back at how I approached this season with eyes wide open but, by the time the year ended, I was broken into so many pieces, intentionally suffering.

Through the process, I found that growth is not something that comes without sacrifice. And growth in Christ was not optional for me. Each time I tried to expand and go deeper than before, I hit roadblock after roadblock. God showed me that He couldn't occupy a space that wasn't free, and that's when I realized some things that were a part of me needed to be released. My will for my life, generational curses, laziness, lust, pride, all of the counterfeit pieces…everything in me that was not like God had to go. My heart and mind had to be unoccupied for Him to inhabit it, and that meant reprioritizing my life. It meant committing my time to our relationship, being content with staying still, and it meant A LOT of failures and teaching moments.

While making space for Him, He put me in an intentionally single season. So, beyond the general cleaning of house that I was doing, He didn't want me pursuing any man but Him. He knew that in the pursuit of Him, I could find me. What I didn't know at the time was this was the start of my disassembly.

When I started studying for my degree in Theological Studies in 2019, I determined what things/events I could sacrifice to spend more intentional time with God, and I set out to know Him on a deeper level. But heaven didn't open, and miracles didn't fall down on my life the more time I spent with Him. The exact opposite in fact. The chambers opened and pieces buried within pieces of me started being unveiled, and it was not pretty. On top of my personal issues, my world at church got shaken up, which disturbed the very ground that my foundation started to be rebuilt on. This is not what I asked for or pictured for this year. I imagined making space for God in my life would look like a love story. It didn't. It looked like a horror film in which I was the dumb, main character causing my own demise because I was chasing the right thing. I was chasing God and it still seemed to result in destruction. This is when I started to learn what healing actually looked like, and it doesn't start with mending, no matter how broken you might feel like you already are. God can't fix what *He* hasn't broken. And while there were a lot of broken pieces in my life, it was me who broke them, not God. This kind of breaking cannot mean cracking on the surface but completely broken and torn apart so that you can dissect and reassess

> **This is when I started to learn what healing actually looked like, and it doesn't start with mending, no matter how broken you might feel like you already are.**

the pieces.

So "space" is what He asked for and that's what I gave Him. I remember being right in the middle of my social media ministry where I was regularly doing live videos and making Instagram posts sharing different lessons that God was teaching me. I knew that God wasn't just teaching me things so I could learn myself, I just knew He wanted me to share it with others. And one day, God just said "Stop." Not that what I was doing was wrong, but it wasn't in proper timing. The lessons were valuable but if I was going to be a vessel that brought His Word to His people, I needed to be an open and healed vessel. And there was still so much stuff muddying the waters. To God, I imagine that I looked like a toddler offering someone their lollipop that just fell on the floor. The offer was driven by the best of intentions, kindness, and innocence; but that doesn't change the fact that it was still gross. I needed cleansing first.

Despite my recommitment and word for the year, I fell down so many times. Hard. After a year of re-committing my purity, I had sex again. After saying I wanted to make space for Him, weeks would go by without me even touching my Bible. I struggled with loneliness that drove me to neglect what He wanted from me and pursue what I wanted for my life again. So many failures created so many reasons to just give up on this pursuit because it was too hard. Like in the past, I've pursued Him and failed to remain committed and consistent every time.

This was something that I struggled with my entire life and one of the main things that's held me back from progress was the idea that I can only fail God so many times. Honestly, I think a huge reason behind the idea that God's grace has limits comes from legalism in some Christian denominations that push the "rules" and potential consequences of them as a key part in understanding God. You grow up thinking that God's only pleased with you if you don't break His rules, and when you do you have to sit down and bear any consequences coming your way. This idea that you need to be sat down or sit out of something and reflect on what you've done doesn't act as a catalyst for growth; it actually does the opposite. You can't make forward progress sitting down. When God sits you down, that's a different story, but this "limited grace" mentality that comes from the church establishes what your concept of forgiveness from God is.

When I was a freshman in college, I got an eyebrow piercing (I could not have been more of a stereotype). My mom was not happy about it (or my belly button piercing) and neither was my pastor at the time. I remember going home for the summer and going back to my home church with it in, just knowing I was going to get the side-eye, but I didn't really care. I was trying to figure out who I wanted to be and, at the time, that eyebrow piercing was a part of that. Before going off to college, I helped with the offering at my church. At the end of service, I'd help the Deacon collect and count the money so that we could announce to the church what the offering was for that Sunday. I was able to do the offering on that first Sunday that I came home but after that service, my Pastor pulled me aside and asked me (very politely) to take the eyebrow ring out before the next service. She didn't approve of it and she didn't think that it was a good representation of the church. If I didn't take it out, I wouldn't be able to continue my duties and help with the offering. What she had disapproved of and classified as sin disqualified me from being able to serve in my church. I had to sit down.

Let's be clear, it was not sin. God couldn't care less about my eyebrow ring, but she was very conservative

(I mean like, you HAD to wear panty hose to church, conservative) and, like most conservative Christians, took Leviticus 19:28 out of context. As harmless as this seems, it was just one example of how my understanding of the "rules" was formed and it taught me that if I don't obey them, I could be disqualified from a place in the Body of Christ.

So, for years, I had struggled with the idea I had gone too far and done too much wrong to be able to walk in my calling. So here I was again, trying to pursue God and a real relationship with Him and failing yet again. My misconception of His grace made me think I had run out of chances but, in a turn of events, God introduced me to the definition of His love, grace, and forgiveness through His Word. When I set out to start reading the Bible again, I started in the New Testament even though I was always taught that you should read the Bible in order (I do not know why some churches teach this, some books aren't even placed in chronological order). I thought that I made this decision because the New Testament was so much more interesting and relevant than the Old Testament. What I know now is that God needed me to learn His love and grace through the example of Jesus before learning about anything else.

As I began to read the Gospels in totality, and not just bits and pieces like I had done before, I started seeing a theme of failure from the disciples. For anyone who's never read the Gospels in the Bible (Matthew, Mark, Luke & John) failure is not the intended message or summary of them; this is just what God needed me to see. The disciples that were hand-selected by Jesus Himself failed him, consistently. Through their entire time with Jesus, while He was in His earthly ministry, they kept letting Him down. They lacked faith, they misunderstood so much of what He was trying to teach them, they betrayed Him, denied Him, and the list goes on. These holy men that founded the Church and spread the Gospel from Jerusalem, Judea, Samaria, and to all the ends of the earth were human…just like me, and they were still chosen, called, and appointed. Through their failures and lack of faith, Jesus never turned His back on them once. He never disqualified them for the task at hand, and He never thought their failure wasn't worth dying for. After learning that their walk with Christ didn't look like rainbows and perfection, but it looked very similar to mine, I started to understand God's grace a little bit. What it taught me was that God was never looking for perfection from me, He just wanted effort. And there was nothing that I could do while on this earth that could disqualify me from the calling that God placed on my life. I just needed to keep getting up whenever I fell.

In the height of my disastrous year, while I was trying to make space for God, He helped me truly understand His love and His grace. I think that when you go to church all of your life the idea of His love and grace is just known. Sometimes it's felt by His presence resting on you, but your confidence in the fact that God loves you is because that's what you've always been taught. So, the idea that I didn't really know His love and His grace seems so weird, but it was true. After learning that I could fall countless times and still get up and be used by God, He solidified the extent of His grace and just how much He loves me in Romans chapters 7-8.

Paul, who is arguably one of the most important figures in Christian history, wrote about God's love and grace, and I believe He did it specifically for me. Throughout chapter 7 of Romans, Paul is dwelling on the battle that Christians endlessly face where we want so badly to please God, but our flesh also has a strong desire to be pleased. He says this in Romans 7:21-23: "So I find this law at work: Although I want to do good, evil is right there with me. For my inner being I delight in God's law; but I see another law at work in me, waging war against the law of my mind and making me a prisoner of the law of sin at work within me" (NIV). I had never connected with something more than this sonnet written by Paul. And it was so timely. I wanted so badly to pursue the Kingdom of God and shed the things holding me back from who He needs me to be, but the law was at work in me waging war against what my flesh wanted. My heart, mind, and flesh were all at war, and I didn't know how to win the war that was happening inside of me. BUT

...through Christ Jesus the law of the Spirit who gives life has set you free from the law of sin and death. For what the law was powerless to do because it was weakened by the flesh, God did by sending his own Son in the likeness of sinful flesh to be a sin offering. And so, He condemned sin in the flesh, in order that the righteousness requirement of the law might be fully met in us, who do not live according to the flesh but according to the Spirit (Romans

81

8:2-4, NIV).

So, you're telling me that God knows that I'm powerless to my flesh? You're telling me that He never intended me to fight it? You're telling me that His plan for my life always included my failures, and that's why He sent His Son to die for me and then His Spirit to guide me? God didn't intend for His children to wrestle with the fact that we sin. He didn't intend for the very idea of our failures to be yet another roadblock that keeps us from Him. He didn't just die to cover the sin; it was to cover the guilt and shame of it too. It's likely that I heard this many times before in sermons from various preachers or ministers, but it never clicked until I read this scripture for myself. God called me to righteousness, but He sent His Spirit to do the righteousness part for me 😌. This is the equivelant of a teacher handing you a test and a cheat sheet at the same time. You have to do the work but there's a guide to help you through it. All you have to do is acknowledge that guide. Now the "rules" couldn't bind me anymore because I know that I'm not subject to them. I'm subject to the law of the Spirit and led into the sonship of Christ (Romans 8:14, NIV) <Exit pressure, guilt, shame, and unworthiness>. I didn't know that I was loved, and I could have never imagined I was loved that much. I didn't know that I was created with a purpose that couldn't be destroyed by my own power and stupidity. The pressure to not fail had cultivated failure and shame because of it. But now, there's no pressure to not fail, because God knows I will, and He still loves me. And beyond that, after my failure, He's the one to dust me off and send me off to the next step in my journey. My failure doesn't catch Him by surprise, He's merely waiting for me to realize I'm already forgiven and get back up so we can keep going. There's no condemnation in my failure because of His Spirit.

Y'all, I found love for the first time. I mean, real love: sacrificial, grace-filled, and fully supportive love. To this day, these chapters in Romans read as a love letter to me. God sent His Son because of my future sin. What I may do tomorrow isn't new to Him, it's only new to me. This Man died on a cross to save me from the sins I don't even know I'm going to commit tomorrow; I mean, He just covered it all. And then, to top it off, He KNOWS I'm always going to stumble so He removes the constraints of the law and sends a guiding Spirit to lead me to the righteousness that the law requires. It's such a protective, forgiving, and proven love that I didn't know God had given me. All along, there was freedom from those counterfeit pieces through His love and grace. It wasn't something that I had to wait until I got older to walk in; it just took genuine knowledge, understanding of it, and faith to believe it. But I didn't know His love before, so how could it have freed me?

Although I felt like so much destruction was happening while I was making space for Him, soooo much growth was happening that I couldn't see. And that destruction, it was intentional. After learning about this beautiful love that I'm given, with no conditions, the shame and unworthiness left. The counterfeit pieces were gone and there was space for God to occupy me. Because, what's there to be ashamed of? The mistakes that I've made, and continue to make, were fully known by Jesus when He died on the cross centuries ago. These mistakes are only new to me so why should I feel ashamed about them? He knew all that I would do and still decided to call me His. He still decided to call me to ministry. He still decided to love me. I didn't earn any of it, so how could anything I did disqualify me from it?

When the enemy can't destroy, he distracts. It's

another trick of his. He **66 When the enemy can't destroy, he distracts. 99** will come at you and challenge your availability to God and your visibility to His grace. I was distracted for years by shame and unworthiness that told me I would never be good enough. As a result, I could never feel and believe the magnitude with which God loved me. But, with the removal of those pieces, a new picture is starting to make its way through. Now that I'm fully confident in His love and the fact that I have purpose, I'm seeing an image from the scattered pieces.

I started writing this book on Jan. 12th, 2019, at the start of my disassembly. When God told me to write it, I wrote His instructions in my journal and wrote down "write the book because of 1 John 2:12; people need to know." 1 John 2:12 reads "I am writing to you, dear children, because your sins have been forgiven on account of His name" (NIV). I didn't know this at the time, but God was telling me that so I could first believe the scripture for myself and then write about my experience to help others believe it.

2019 marked the year of making space for God. I had to clear out anything that wasn't relevant to my progress to make more time for God. As I started intentionally making space for Him, I began the disassembly process of my puzzle and started on a journey that I didn't realize I signed up for. What I found was that when you remove things that don't belong, it leaves behind an empty space to be filled. I didn't know that I signed up for God to break me and destroy the image that I knew so He could finally reveal His masterpiece. But that's what was happening, and I was not a consenting party. I had to start building a relationship with myself, forgiving myself, and loving myself. I had to find a way to love every broken piece that, to my own fault, was defective. And I had to forgive myself for the defective pieces.

In a commencement speech at the University of Houston, Matthew McConaughey said, "Knowing who we are is hard. Eliminate who you are NOT first, and you'll find yourself where you need to be."

DADDY ISSUES

---

dad·dy is·sues
/ˈdadē ˈiSHoos/

noun

1. when a child has a bad or absent relationship with
a birth parent, resulting in unconscious psycholog-
ical problems

Daddy issues is a modern term used to describe
lingering issues in someone's life because of an
absent parent. Also known by some as "Father Com-
plex." In my case, it's a very literal phrase since the
lingering issues in my life were actually issues caused
by my absent father.

Ever since I can remember, I've been waiting for
prince charming. It's like my life was built around
it. Everything that I went through, everything that I
achieved, was all leading up to the moment that a man

would walk into my life and be my knight in shining armor. He'd come into my life and stay, no matter what. He'd fight for me and show me that I was worth the fight. He'd be a partner, a friend, a refuge, and a confidant. I can literally remember thoughts of this dream before I had even hit puberty. My life was built on it.

A husband and a marriage were the goal. Not really for any vain reasons like being desired, but for security reasons like "someone always has my back." I've pined after this goal for years, desperately awaiting the day that would start the rest of my life. When I'd question myself about why I wanted this so badly, I just always assumed that God gave me this burning passion to be married and be a helpmate to someone. I have so much love to give and so much of me to offer, it had to be God that gave me the desire to give it away, right?

Wrong. At 27 I was established in my career, financially stable, and active in church with only the hopes of marriage in sight when God put me in a single season so I could grow close to Him. Let's get a little perspective and remember that I was a girl who had previously been sexually active, and I was being asked to not only live pure but be single. I had to submit what I wanted to get what I needed. This was a direct result of watching the sermon series Relationship Goals by Pastor Mike Todd. The first sermon in the series was the set up for how we should approach relationships. First, we must love God, then ourselves, and only then can we accurately love others. He also reviewed what should happen within you before your person comes along so that you're not bringing singleness issues into a relationship and calling it relationship issues. I realized through this series, God was trying to get me to build a foundation on Him and not a person. If I don't find love for myself or set my success on the love of another person, my life then becomes dependent on that person. If God were to send me someone before I filled my void with His love, simply because I'm lonely, he then becomes a temporary fix and still can't truly fill my void. If I'm insecure and He sends someone to make me feel pretty, I'm masking that insecurity instead of healing it, and it will come out in new forms in that relationship. So, there was some work to be done in my single season.

After walking through this series and realizing that I was FAR from being able to be in a healthy relationship, I set out to discover my identity and discover God's purpose for me in my singleness. By seeking

Him and consuming myself with His Word and His work, I was able to put my desperate feelings of marriage on the back burner. In doing so, they came back up to the forefront of my mind sporadically and repeatedly. To my understanding, I just needed to fight through this until God declares me fit and sends my husband. So begins my fight with loneliness and the reason for my relapses in purity while I was making space for God. I fought thoughts of being alone and the idea that I didn't deserve God's best, because I still so desperately wanted what I just couldn't have at that time.

This wasn't a feeling unfamiliar to me though. I've been wanting to be married basically my entire life, so I'm no stranger to feeling alone. But what I realized is that this "God-given" desire to be married so badly was actually a desire to be loved. Even now, it's really hard to admit this to myself because I've ALWAYS been loved. My mom, my family, and God – I've always had consistent and real love from these sources. But even still, I desired love from a man, an unconditional and unchangeable love that would always be there and never leave. Why? Because my heart is scarred from the irregular, inconsistent, wishy-washy, conditional, optional love that I received from my dad. God showed me that my heart was wounded in a way that only allowed me to see symptoms of the wound. The only problems that I knew I had to fix were the addictions that manifested themselves out of the invisible wound, but if you had asked me, I was fine. My heart was fine. I would have told you that I had completely forgiven my father for not being in my life and I've moved on to a healthy place. I hadn't considered the fact that as a father, he was obligated to give me something and, even though I've released him of his responsibilities, the transfer that should have occurred didn't, so I will forever be in void of something until I seek what can permanently fill it. My heart was wounded and scarred deeper than what I could heal through forgiveness.

Those heart wounds manifested themselves as addictions, desperation, and overcompensation. I just HAD to find someone and, when I did, I just HAD to show them that I would do ANYTHING in the world for them to get them to stay. I had to prove that I was worth someone sticking around. I had to feel like I was someone's number 1 priority. But even this symptom of my daddy issues manifested itself as something else. It came off like "I just have a lot to offer and I expect

91

the same in return." It showed itself as a quality, not an issue. So, in my bad relationships, I always thought the guy was the issue: he's not good enough, he doesn't put in the effort or he won't be able to meet my needs. And while most of the time that was true, the reality is that the slightest inconvenience to me in a relationship would cause me to jump ship so that I could leave before he had the opportunity to leave me. Honestly, this manifested itself in all of my relationships, romantic or not. I'm careful about how much of myself I invest into people and I'm quick to pull away if they're not giving the same effort.

It's hard to love people like Jesus does. People hurt you, they neglect you, and they use you. When you put your all into something or someone and you sacrifice so much to be there for people, they often don't make the same sacrifices. This led to me treating people like they're disposable. The world will have us believe that we shouldn't care about others in the same way that we care about ourselves and, at some point, you can give up on them, but this is another trick of the enemy. People aren't disposable. Jesus proved that. Philippians 2:3 says, "Rather, in humility, value others above yourselves, not looking to your own interests but each of you to the interests of others" (NIV). There was this huge hole in my heart that was longing to be filled, and it was distorting my idea of how to love others and myself. There are wounds that want healing and I have abandonment scars that won't allow me to fight for connections with people—Daddy issues.

But beyond my general love for people, my daddy issues manifested in my romantic relationships too. The longest relationship that I've ever had was with a guy that we're going to call Ryan. He and I met online in 2016 during the height of my shame, and I was using online dating as a coping mechanism. He and I dated for about a year and a half, and then I called it quits in late 2017, just as I started to realize who I was again. I had so much love for him. He was funny, fun to be around, charming, inquisitive, ambitious, loving, athletic, handsome, and his shining attribute was his love for God. Our relationship started after he took notice of my love for God; that's what connected us. The beginning stages of our relationship were like most, I was completely smitten. The honeymoon phase had me convinced that this was the love of my life, and I could see myself settling down with him. During this phase, he was a perfect gentleman who gave me the love that I never had from a man. It was a present, unconditional, and caring kind of love. The honeymoon phase ended when the conditions came. This conditional love was something that I had seen before from my dad, and when it starts to manifest itself in other people, I run. The type of love he was giving me changed, and I had no idea why at the time. The façade of sweetness was gone, and he started showing me that his intentions were decent but never backed by action. He would tell me one thing and then do another. Everything we did was on his terms, and he'd always make happy occasions sad for me, including his birthday and my own birthday. He always found a way to make me sad and didn't really seem to care, so I concluded that this wasn't love and I broke it off.

An entire year after we broke up, I found myself still involved with him, mostly in a sexual way. I had a very hard time letting him go because, after we broke up, he was persistent in pursuing me and he was always around because he did, in fact, love me. What I've learned is that the way people were shown or not shown love is the way that they give it to others. What he was giving me didn't feel like love, but I know now that it's the only way he knew how to love. I, on the other hand, tried to love him by giving him all of me. I put my all into trying to make him happy, because, to me, love needed to be proven worthy of. I had to prove that I was worth his love, so I depleted everything in me to make sure he knew. When that wasn't reciprocated or even noticed, I concluded that he didn't love me. He had no idea that my version of love was shaped by absence, conditions, and irregularity which made me need to see consistency, action, and presence, especially when I'm doing so much to prove that I'm worth that.

At the time, I thought that he wasn't a good guy. I thought that he was too self-absorbed to love me right, and he didn't know how to be in a relationship. Some of that is true but I realized that it wasn't to the magnitude that I thought. See, I thought that, overtime, his ability to love me right disintegrated, but that wasn't true at all. The truth was that he never loved me the way I needed to be loved from the beginning and, to my surprise, it wasn't his fault. My desperation to keep him by doing anything I could to make him happy overshadowed the fact that my needs were never met. For over a year, I was content with bare minimum effort from him, not being able to spend quality time together and not feeling like I was a part of his life, despite attempts to tell him how I felt. This contentment held me down while I was still pressing to give him my all. I think what happened was I ran out of me to give. What I needed wasn't being replenished, so what I had to give came to an abrupt end. That's when the relationship began to spiral. That's when I started feeling like I was in it alone and needed to let it go. And when I finally did, I was convinced that he wasn't the one. Now, looking back, I realize that he was never the one from the very beginning. He didn't have an opportunity to understand or prioritize my needs because I didn't prioritize them myself. I showed him how to love me. I didn't take my own needs seriously by putting me first, so he didn't either. But hindsight is 2020.

After our breakup, he continued to tell me he loved me. And he showed it even more now, so I clung to this. I clung to the idea that, despite my rejection of him and claiming that I don't love him anymore, he loves me. It started to feel like unconditional love again. The idea that he loved me, and he would always be there because he loved me, made me hold on to him when I should have let him go. It made me cling on to his love and my love for him began to rise again. So, years after we broke up, he was still heavily in my life. He offered me the security that I always wanted: to feel like a man would be there, unconditionally. But it wasn't fair for me to keep him in my life for my security. It wasn't fair for him or for me. I knew that we weren't supposed to be together, and I knew that I did not want to be in a relationship with him again, but I started to love the way he loved me. This is where it became detrimental; he couldn't heal because I was stringing him along, and I couldn't trust God to provide a husband for me because I had a backup plan. Holding on to Ryan was another symptom of my wounds, and I didn't even know it.

From 2017 to 2019, I had so many on and off friendships/situationships with him. I would block him, months would go by, and I would miss his friendship, so I'd unblock him. Things would start back up again. Then, he would do something to remind me that he's not who I'm supposed to be with, and I'd block him again. Two years I existed in this cycle with him. My hope was always to just have him in my life as a friend, because he was truly my best friend at the time (and I was lonely) but no matter what, neither of us could help but fall back into the romantic cycle. So, time after time, God would tell me to let it go for my own good, but his absence would start to become more painful than the shockingly poor form of love that he tried to show me, so I always let him back in. It's amazing what we're willing to settle for when we've not healed from past pain.

In every attempt to let him go by blocking him, I would tell God that I was ready to be married now. "Ryan's out; You can send my husband now." But He never did. This is what made it so hard to keep Ryan out. While he was blocked, and God wasn't showing any signs of sending my boo, I was alone. I'm an introvert so I prefer being alone as opposed to being around a ton of people but being alone with someone I loved was my preference.

It's amazing what we're willing to settle for when we've not healed from past pain.

Loneliness wasn't painful or hard because of the lack of someone else's presence. It was challenging because it amplified my own presence, my issues, and my pain. So, "God, send him…please!!" was my consistent cry. "I'm ready to get my life started with that special one!" Man, I would shout this and feel like it was hitting a brick wall. Crickets, dead silence, and probably even laughter was all I got back. The fact that God didn't send someone for me when I was lonely made me feel even more abandoned. This just magnified how alone I was and the idea that marriage was the way out.

June 25th, 2019—this day marked freedom from an invisible chain that broke the bondage of the daddy issues I had and my need for marriage, which we'll talk about more in a few chapters. One of the hardest things about growth is fixing problems that you didn't know were there or asking God to heal areas that you didn't know needed healing. The simple discovery of that chain broke the bondage of it. Just after my 28th birthday, God revealed to me wounds that I had on my heart that drove lust, the overeager desperation to be married, and horrible coping mechanisms. You all found out in chapter 1, but I didn't know until chapter 28 of my life that I had a void in my heart and that, left untreated, manifested into daddy issues that helped shape how I loved and what I so desperately desired from a man. I simply didn't know.

But what I learned was that marriage isn't the cure for my abandonment issues and marriage won't help me feel the love that my dad should have poured into me. Had it not been for divine revelation, I would still be walking into platonic and romantic relationships seeking things from people that only God can give me.

ALONE

a·lone
/ ə'lōn/

adjective

1. having no one else present

For the entire year of 2019, I was alone. Yes, Ryan was in my life here in there but never for more than a few weeks at a time. Other than that, I was alone, alone. Whoever said "just because I'm alone doesn't mean that I'm lonely" was not speaking for all of us. I was alone and lonely, and I didn't understand how someone could not feel lonely while being alone. This journey of dismantling the picture of my life has been so beautiful but ugly at the same time. I see so many things that I don't like in me, so many things that are not like God, so many things that a lifetime couldn't fix, and so many things that I don't want to even face.

Honestly, it made me feel hopeless. There was so much I didn't like. The work that needed to be done was intense, and I was no Bob the Builder.

Being alone while making space so God could have more of me was like watching a horror movie alone. You're just bound to be afraid, pee yourself, and be riddled with anxiety throughout the movie, but you indulge anyway and end up with immediate regret. I'm alone and I'm not happy. I'm frustrated. I'm angry. I feel lost, abandoned, and I'm afraid. Also, I didn't have the old friends that helped me get through my adolescence. God had healed me from those counterfeit pieces that were familiar, so I couldn't even find comfort in that. 2019 showed me the worst of me. It showed me my desperation, it showed me strongholds that I mistook for simple barriers, and it showed me that I had a lot of work to do on me before bringing my broken pieces into someone else's life. Each time I came face to face with a new piece of the puzzle, I felt an overwhelming sense of "Oh God, there's more?!" It got to the point where it became harder to want progress; I just wanted to be content with who I was in that moment for the rest of my life. I think the hardest thing that I had to learn about myself was the fact that I found it hard for me to love me. My loneliness was the manifestation of lack of love for myself.

I saw a meme on Instagram that said the most complicated relationship you will ever have is with yourself, and it's because you can't walk away from you. You have to forgive every mistake and deal with every single one of your flaws. You have to find a way to love you, even when you're disgusted with you. You can't love God and not love what He created. But, I did. My past was riddled with sin, shame, and failure after failure, and it turned into flaws and distain for what I had done to me. Even after the shame left, the scars of the pain I had caused were still there. When God showed me His grace, I forgave myself, but I never forgot. It was in the same way you can forgive an ex for hurting you and have no hatred towards them but know better than to try to love them

> ❝ **The most complicated relationship you will ever have is with yourself, and it's because you can't walk away from you. You have to forgive every mistake and deal with every single one of your flaws. You have to find a way to love you, even when you're disgusted with you. You can't love God and not love what He created.** ❞

again. I think that's how I felt about me. I forgave me but didn't want to give me another try; I was good. I walked away from me, and God was calling me back to His creation. He was asking, no, telling me, to work it out with me. Because if I can't love His creation, how could I love His people? And if I can't love His people, how could I really love Him?

Loneliness forced me into couples counseling with myself. It happened in a few stages. First, was resistance, then submersion but not submission, depression, coping, acceptance, submission, and then harvest.

After I accepted being alone and discovered that I did not like it or myself, I resisted hard. My resistance came very indirectly, because it didn't seem like I was resisting. It seemed like I had accepted it. I was in a singleness season, and I told myself that it was going to be a short season and all I had to do was make it through. I needed to put my feelings and desires on the back burner for now so I could concentrate on God. I didn't realize that this temporary solution I gave myself was resistance to the truth. I was able to shift my focus away from a desire to be married so I could grow my relationship with God, but it was temporary. The truth it resisted was that this season was never intended to be a short-lived honeymoon with me and God. It was intended to help me destroy a lot of the foreign pieces in my puzzle. But I resisted a deeper level of growth initially. I think it was because I knew going deeper would mean being alone longer and that was not really in the cards. So, I sat on the surface of my single season, temporarily putting my desires for love and marriage on the back burner while I tried to focus on God. That "focus" led me to submersion.

I didn't know this at the time, but I submerged myself into my relationship with God while not having actually submitted yet. The difference? I filled my void with the things of God as a temporary measure to what my real joy and happiness would be, which was love and marriage. The craziest part about it is that God didn't reject that time I gave Him; He took it and gave it a lifetime value. Submersion for me looked like drowning myself in serving at church, faithfully attending and leading an eGroup, and starting my ministry online. Don't get me wrong; God valued all of these things. Honestly, it was exactly what I was supposed to be doing. But the reason that I say this was submersion and not submission is because my intention behind a lot of these things came from a place of distraction from my loneliness vs. genuine desire to do it. *While I wait for this single season to be over, let me drown myself in all things God and fill up every minute that I have so I don't have to think about how hard it is to wait on God, alone.* Submersion got hard because my heart wasn't all the way in it. Most of the time I was thinking about the fact that if I just make it through this hard part, God will bless me with what I want. But God didn't want that. He didn't want half of my attention and He didn't want me to seek Him only so I could get something in return. He wanted all of me. He wanted me to want Him and love Him simply for who He is, not just what He can do. When you seek God solely for the purpose of fulfilling your agenda, you'll end up believing that God doesn't hear you or that He wants you to suffer should your agenda not be satisfied. This is what led me to depression.

Depression crept up on me. It wasn't an all at once thing. It started when the things I had submerged myself in started to recede, leaving me exposed. I was submerged in service at my church for months, and then, all of a sudden, I wasn't anymore. Things changed and people left. Literally, everyone. All of the people I had been doing life with, who were anchors in my submersion... left. And while it might sound like I'm exaggerating, I'm not. Most people moved away, and some went to a different church, but over the course of about 2-3 months everyone who was important to me was gone out of my life. With their departure, a new regime entered at church, which led me to step down from my leadership position. So then, I was single, friendless, and without a community. I was the loneliest alone I had ever been. So naturally, I was angry. I got mad at the people and circumstances that forced my normalcy out the door, and I started fighting things that weren't the real battle. My focus was on the rain that came to drown me, and I lost sight of the fact that I could swim. Looking back now, I see that God could not grow me while I was in my comfort zone. If I was attached to the people, the place, or what we were doing, I would never become attached to Him or His promise. I'd never wholeheartedly seek out His desires for me outside of the comfort of the community that gave me purpose. In that season, when everything

My focus was on the rain that came to drown me, and I lost sight of the fact that I could swim.

shifted and God yanked my crutches from under my arms, I fell. I had no idea why He'd stop me dead in the middle of my service to Him, or why He'd stop a group of people so desperately chasing after Him and ready to shake up a city together. He completely re-routed me in the most abrupt way, and I was so confused.

The end of 2019 was the absolute hardest season of my singleness. I was so sad all the time. I was doing life alone, and I was even more sad now because it seemed like God wanted me to be alone. Most of my hill tops started to not feel as worth it as they should, and all of my valleys were worsened by the lack of someone to share it with. It started to pain me seeing everyone I knew get everything that I wanted, and I mean everyone. It was almost like God was taunting me and I couldn't understand why. I spent a lot of nights crying, trying to wrap my head around why God was singling me out and making me suffer. A part of me thought that, maybe, God just wants me for Himself. I had given myself to the world for most of my life, maybe He just wants to be with me now. But if that's true, why won't He take the pain away. Why won't He just take away my desire to see marriage and have a love here on this earth? Why would He allow our time together to feel so bad? Why won't He just remove this deep-seeded desire to fill my void with a husband?

One night, as I was crying and begging God for what I thought was going to fill my void, I wrote down my broken-hearted prayer to God:

"Jesus, I hate this season of my life that I've been asked to endure alone. It's so hard to find comfort in You when you're the One asking me to do what makes me so uncomfortable and so unhappy. It's hard to seek You right now, and it's hard to trust You. I just want the loneliness and the pain to end. I'm being asked to choose between You and the human nature that You gave me, and I just don't understand why You would give me the desires if You didn't want me to have these things. I'm at a crossroads. I have no idea what to do, because You won't help me love You better by just taking this loneliness away. It's so painful watching You move everyone else's mountain and knowing You can do it, but You won't move mine."

This was a prayer of pain, of heartache, and of fatigue. I was tired of fighting my own desires for His. I was tired of being alone. This depression made me develop coping mechanisms for the pain.

109

The coping mechanism didn't start during this loneliness season, but it came in strong around this time. Over the last 2 years, I buried so much pain and frustration with my life, the journey to redemption, and with God, that I created my own escape. Most addictions come from a person trying to fill a void or mask pain, and I was trying to do both. Our bodies weren't meant to just accept pain. This is why people pass out if the pain is too severe; it's our body's coping mechanism and escape from enduring the pain. My escape was similar. I was depressed but still 100% committed to growing in God and my purity. My escape was very legal and not as cliché as sex or alcohol but just as damaging, because it turned into an addiction.

Sleep was my coping mechanism. Escaping my pain by going to bed was something that started so discreetly and innocently, but it developed into a habit so fast that I didn't realize I was addicted until I came out of it. As long as I had taken care of what I needed to for the day, I could go to bed as early as 6pm and just sleep until the next day, escaping from a reality that I didn't want to face: that I was alone and I hated it.

Benadryl, Nyquil, Melatonin, and Tylenol PM became my way of escape and the only real thing to look forward to after work. If I had to be alone, I didn't want to endure the pain of it. It started out as a once in a while thing, then once a week, and then I couldn't go to bed without taking something. Benadryl and Tylenol PM would knock me out cold, and I wouldn't have to deal with lonely nights. Honestly, this habit would have never stopped if I didn't realize how it was affecting my health. After a few years of being addicted to sleeping medicine, I realized that it was leading to me developing health issues that I shouldn't have allowed. First, I found out that I had gallstones. These are stones in your gallbladder that cause severe pain. Depending on how big your stones are, the pain can be chronic and stop you from eating or doing regular day to day things. For me, the pain was severe enough that I couldn't eat for days, and I was in consistent pain for over a week. When it finally got bad enough, I went to the ER and that's where I was diagnosed. Typically, the recommendation with gallstones is to have your entire gallbladder removed, which is what I had done. Your gallbladder is a body part that you can live without, but your body definitely has to do some adjustments post removal. In addition to body adjustments, you get a nice little hospital bill. I know now that this was completely avoidable, and I, in a sense, did this to myself.

The next issue that it led to was significant weight gain. I'm not a terrible eater and I'm active (in a non-couch potato sense) but, all of a sudden, I was gaining a ton of weight. I couldn't understand why or get the weight off. My normal diets weren't working, and exercise wasn't doing a thing. I started to believe that the aging process was changing my body beyond my control. I don't remember why (looking back now, it was probably God) but one week, I went a few nights without taking any sleep aides. It felt really good to not need anything. The next week after that, I felt lighter, like I had lost a few pounds. As I thought back on what I did differently the previous week, I remembered that I skipped sleeping aids a few nights, so I tried that again and discovered a lot about how it had been affecting me. It turned out that hard sleeping aids like Benadryl and Tylenol PM block your histamine receptors – histamine is a chemical that regulates your food intake. Basically, it tells you when you're full. Blocking that receptor with those aides makes you hungry, even if you are in fact full. When I was taking these sleeping aids daily, I was constantly eating in the middle of the night—sometimes really poor food, but most of the time it was just a snack like Goldfish or crackers. Regardless of the type of food, it was happening daily. I was eating way more than my body needed and eating in the middle of the night for the food to just sit inside my stomach. This is what caused me to develop gallstones, which I could only cure by getting surgery to remove my gallbladder. This is also what caused my significant weight gain even after the surgery.

My coping mechanism drove me to become the unhealthiest version of myself that I had ever been. I was wasting away, and I began hating myself. I felt useless to God because I didn't think I was strong enough to do what He needed me to do. I wasn't happy, and I was failing in this season. I wanted to continue to pursue what God told me to, but I didn't feel like I had a target anymore. Meanwhile, I still didn't have what I really wanted, which was love. So, what was I fighting for? What was the goal? All it had led me to was depression, addiction, and weight gain. It was these moments that made it so easy for me to run back to Ryan. And I did, multiple times. In trying to figure out how to love myself, I ended up being even more disgusted with myself. So naturally, I need someone else to show me love. I need someone else to give me what I couldn't give myself.

"Don't give up on what you want most for what

you want right now."

That quote was annoying and came right in the middle of this depression, but it led me to acceptance. I know most people look for encouragement and for God to speak to them during tough times, but God saying this to me while I was frustrated with figuring out the puzzle…alone, was just cruel. It didn't feel like help at all. It felt like He was saying "Yes, Tyeisha. I do want you to continue to be in pain while in pursuit of my purpose." My question back to God after He presented me with this quote was "what if the thing I want most IS the thing being offered right now?" I really wanted to share my life with someone and felt like I had an opportunity to do it with Ryan since he welcomed me with open arms every time I ran back to him. I did not trust God to give me the love that I needed. I wanted to secure it for myself.

But then, I remembered (or God decided to slap the silly out of me) the thing that I wanted most, even more than someone to share my life with, was wholeness. There was a reason I started this "puzzling" journey. God showed me my holes, gaps, and broken pieces, and I wanted my puzzle to be made complete. I wanted to be whole. What I wanted right now was just someone to love me because I couldn't figure out how to love myself. I didn't want to sacrifice wholeness, but I didn't want to sacrifice love either. And through resistance, depression, submersion, and coping I felt like I was sacrificing both. It was time to make a decision on which was more important.

"You shouldn't drink poison just because
you're thirsty"

This was the second quote that came around the same time and helped make my decision clear. I was truly thirsty for love, but that didn't mean I needed to settle. God showed me I'm worth suffering and dying for. And if He thinks that much of me, I have to figure out how to love me at the same level. In order to do that, I have to rid myself of the desire to fill my void with man's love. My heart was desperate for love from God and love from myself, not anyone else. And through this love was where I could find wholeness. So, how do we prioritize wholeness? Submission, not submersion.

In order to submit, you have to let go of what you want and actually believe that God has something better for you; you also have to believe that you're worth the

115

better that He has. We lose our sense of worth through years of shame and condemnation, but God didn't send that. If you don't restore your sense of worth, your image of yourself reflects on to how God feels about you, and it's hard to believe that He has great things in store for you if you feel like you don't deserve it. Submission means laying down your will for your life, not just putting it on the back burner. It's tearing up the story that you wrote in your mind of how your life would go; it's allowing God to remove pieces of your puzzle that you were attached to, because they don't fit the picture He's trying to make. Submission is HARD. Mostly because you won't really know if you've submitted until you're tested. You can tell God all day "Your will God, not mine" but it's not until He says that His will is for you to leave the job you've been at for 15 years, or to be alone when all of your scars come from abandonment, that you'll be able to see if you've really laid down what you want for what He has for you.

Submission is a requirement for God to work in you. His spirit can't operate in a vessel that has not humbled itself to what He wants. If you haven't submitted yourself or your plans to Him or His will, you cannot physically obey. I had to learn this the hard way. Your plans will always come to the forefront and lead to disobedience, no matter how hard you try to listen to what God is saying, if you have not submitted. When you're operating under your own will, His voice becomes completely still. It's loud and fully functional in HIS will, but your voice is the loudest in your will. Greater heights call for greater sacrifice. At this level, I was sacrificing what I thought I needed and who I wanted to be; this was necessary for God to make me into who He needed me to be.

So, what do you do when God tells you to submit yourself and your plan to Him and, out of negligence or complete disobedience, you don't? The enemy will challenge you in these moments. He'll challenge you to abort what you know, go back to your old life, or go back to behaviors that make you feel comfortable since you've "failed God". But I promise you, the stretching, the beating, and the pressing is all for your good. It may not feel like it, and it WILL feel out of place, but it's all for His good and His plan. His plan for you includes your failures. Learn from this lesson and press forward towards submission, knowing that what you want for your life could never amount to what God has planned. Submission was a feeling at first. And then, it became a seed, which led to a harvest.

I've coped with loneliness for most of my life. It has always been minimized by distractions. In this season, God intentionally manifested my loneliness so I could see the lack of love for myself. He also maximized the depths of the addictions that left me unsatisfied when the high is gone—still sad, and still alone. I've prayed for healing endlessly but praying for healing for a symptom will only produce a temporary answered prayer. I had to face the real problem. If I let God fix my puzzle how He wants to I'm no longer forcing the image that I want, which only leads to pain and suffering. Allowing His will to manifest in my life allows Him in places that I've never opened to Him before, and it allows Him to fix the broken systems instead of masking the symptoms. When the systems are fixed, you can start producing again and, when you produce, you create a harvest within yourself. From that, you can begin to sow into other people.

66 **Praying for healing for a symptom will only produce a temporary answered prayer.** 99

Paul wrote so many books in the New Testament. Four of those books he wrote in prison. What he taught us is that we have to maximize the time we have in the valley, because the output of that will be a guiding light on the mountain. So, submit to your valley.

> **We have to maximize the time we have in the valley, because the output of that will be a guiding light on the mountain. So, submit to your valley.**

I don't think I'm in love with me, but I do love me now. God literally drug me to this place, kicking and screaming. And when I say "place," I mean process, because, no, I haven't "arrived." I don't think I'll ever be "there," but I've learned that the place of process is the destination. Disassembly and reassembly are my reality and a measurement of success now. To be always "in development" with Him means I've got so far to go, but it also means I've made it.

STRONGHOLDS

---

strong·hold
/ˈstrôNGˌhōld/

noun

1. a place that has been fortified so as to protect it
   against attack

So now, I was in the thick of the process. You know that point where you've already done too much to stop but you're nowhere near close to being finished? Or let me put it another way: I was at the point in my puzzle where I had aligned all of the perimeter pieces and all of the pieces that had objects on them; now it was time to start working on the middle pieces that were just solid colors. No indication about where they should go, no clues, and nothing to confirm that I'm not putting them in the wrong place again with no idea if they belong or not.

The moment you decide to surrender yourself and your will to Him is a surreal moment. You make a decision to include Him in every decision, and you don't make a move without Him. Saying "yes" to God, in the moment, feels great. But that's just a moment. The truth lies in the way that you live that out; it's in the test. And the reality is, during the test, surrendering your will doesn't feel like a burden being lifted. It felt like a fight, like a battle that I was losing. I had surrendered, now what? I let go of my will, my disillusion, my past, my shame, and I was ready to do what He wanted me to do. Do you know what happens next? One would assume it was love, joy, and complete bliss. I could picture God and I skipping down the street holding hands with the song *Reunited* playing in the background. That wasn't my reality, though. My reality, at this point, was more like God and I skipping down the street for 5 seconds, and then I hit a brick wall, but He keeps going. Then, I find my way around it and try to catch up with Him, but a few moments later, I hit another brick wall. These walls aren't just hanging out in my line of sight, they are popping up out of nowhere. What made it even worse is that it felt like God kept going; He kept skipping down the street and every wall set me further and further back from holding hands with Him again.

Cycles like this usually start after your freedom or your surrender. And if it's not the start, then the manifestation of it becomes super visible at this point. Look at the life of David. He slayed Goliath and claimed victory for Israel in a war with the Philistines when he was just a teenager. Then, later in his life, he went on to be King of Israel and known as "the one after God's own heart." That's the part of his life that you typically hear about in sermons: victory over the giant. What most preachers don't labor on is the cycle of war that David existed in with the Philistines after slaying Goliath and even after becoming King. God always saw him through and delivered the enemy into his hands, but right around the corner, there was another war brewing with the same enemy over the same things. And not too long after one victory, David would be right back in the thick of things, fighting the same war.

Your brick wall could be anything—old habits creeping up, lack of growth, not loving people the way you should, and the list goes on. Whatever your brick wall is, it stops you in your forward progression for a while and postpones your progress. The tricky thing about these brick walls is that you're still progressing, so it's not like the voids you had before that would cause you to stand still in that place. You can make forward, consistent progress with these brick walls that pop up out of nowhere, but they slow you down, they distract you, they hurt, and they jeopardize your unity with God.

Those brick walls are called strongholds: a place that has been fortified so as to protect it against attack. The brick wall scene was a place that I was in and, while God was there, it was not His intended place for us to abide together. He created the Garden for our communion. This brick wall scene was a place fortified to protect against attack, so it was prepared to keep me there, no matter what the cost.

My strongholds came in the form of generational curses. It's difficult to even assess the strongholds on your life because they don't show up as things that want to destroy you. They show up as thoughts and behavior that comforts you. Those demons are a friend in your time of need. It's like an opioid addiction. The very thing you're trying to break free from is the only thing that can make you feel better in the moment.

My greatest challenges in my walk with Christ were my desperation to be married and sexual impurity. No matter what, these things followed me. Before I re-committed myself, I struggled. After I re-committed myself, I struggled. While making space for God, I struggled. While being alone, I struggled the most. It didn't matter how much I grew in the knowledge and love of Christ...I struggled. As a part of my puzzle assessment, I dug deep to figure out why I was so desperate to marry someone, why I couldn't be happy with God alone, and why I couldn't shake the bondage of sexual impurity.

God showed me that the desperation to be married came from the void my father left in me that I was actively trying to fill myself. This void, while unique to me, was yet another cycle in my lineage. My sister endured the same void, as did my mom, and her mom. Our unbroken cycles simply lead our next generation to repeat it. My grandmother, my mom, and my sister's unbroken cycle led them to have children at a young age. I, for one, am grateful for that because I wouldn't be here today had my mom not gone through that. However, having children as single mothers at a young age naturally brought some hardships in life. As I reflect on the fact that I was faced with the same challenge of being left with voids and having sex young and out of wedlock, I see how God kept me from the same circumstances. I could have easily repeated the same cycle of having a child young, but it was God who protected me from that. Looking back, I can see that He did that because He knew I was going to be the one to stand up and fight, no matter how hard it was. He needed me to be the generation that broke the curse in our lineage.

Identifying the root and destroying that stronghold wasn't easy, but God allowed me to see the light at the end of that tunnel. But no matter how hard I dug I couldn't get to the root of why sexual impurity had always followed me. I mentioned before that I lost my virginity pretty young, and after that sexual perversion was heightened. In digging deep, I remembered the perversion didn't start after I lost my purity. I could remember having thoughts about sexual encounters when I was a pre-teen. I could even remember inquiring about and seeking to understand the nature of sex when I was 4 or 5. As I tried to comb the memory bank to understand how a 5 year old could know about this, let alone try to understand it, I struggled with a root cause. I never saw it happen when I was little. My mom never talked about it in front of my sister or I, and I wasn't introduced to it by any friends. Yet, I knew about sex and I was curious about it. It felt like I was born into this bondage, well, because... I was. This is what God revealed to me on June 25, 2019. This, my friends, is a generational curse.

Sometimes it's not our past that's keeping us bound; sometimes it's the past of our ancestors. When God revealed this to me, I immediately rejected it. My brain is wired to think that I only suffer the consequences of my own actions. But when a child comes into the world with habits that they couldn't possibly learn in the short amount of time they've been alive, the reality of generational curses become clear. The things that I've learned as I discovered some of my generational curses are,

1. **It's not an oppurtunity to point a finger** - Discovering a generational curse isn't a crutch or cop out. It's a revelation that's supposed to show you how hard you need to fight. The dictionary says that the stronghold is a place that's ready to protect against attack; this means you're not fighting some regular, schmegular demon that you can just cast out. Realizing the difference between a bad habit and a stronghold is critical to determine how to

fight it. But the discovery of a generational curse should never be used to pass blame.

2. The reality is that **even though it's generational, no one is to blame** - God intentionally gives us free will. Everyone has the option to make whatever choice they'd like. It's God's hope that understanding and knowing His love will lead us to good choices, but it doesn't always work that way, and He knows this. The choices that our ancestors made before us were just that...their choices. If this is really a generational curse, God will give you the same oppurtunity to make a choice to fight it. If you decide to not break the chain, God's not going to love you any less. He'll move on and give the next generation the oppurtunity to break the chain. We are not in a place to judge anyone for the decisions that they did or didn't make. We can only be responsible for our own.

3. **God chose me for this very curse** - Before generations before me were given this chain, God knew I'd be in the lineage. I didn't just fall into this stronghold. He chose me for it. And since He chose it for me, I was bound to encounter it at some point in my life. I can't get wrapped up in the idea that if

someone before me had made a different decision, things would be different. What God chose you for is yours and nothing will stop His plan from being carried out.

In a way, I found a sense of freedom through this bondage—kind of like Paul when he was sailing to Rome to be put on trial. He found freedom although he was in chains. I wasn't free yet, but I knew what I was dealing with now, which means I knew how to fight. Now that I know, I have no more excuses. The problems that kept me bound have been uncovered so I have no excuse to not fight. The issue with a lot of our strongholds or giants is that they wear a mask or a cover. And when you don't know what's under the cover, it's hard to pick your weapon. And you don't want to throw all of your weapons at it because that will deplete you. But when the giant is unmasked and you know what you're up against, you now have the intel to determine what you need to fight and defeat it.

Sexual impurity is bondage that a lot of Christians struggle with. It's insane how Satan will take all of the things that God gave us as gifts and pervert them so they work against us. Next to worship, sexuality is the most compromised gift. I remember being at the peak of my impurity, feeling like I wasn't worthy to worship God. The shame of it all overwhelmed me so much so that I gave up my seat in His house; I didn't deserve it. The weight of the struggle took away my ability to fight it for so long. For many years, I just gave in and understood that "that's just who I was." Then, when I did get up the strength to fight it, I'd get knocked back down every time.

For 20+ years these strongholds have gone undetected and seamlessly existed with who I am. These were pieces of my puzzle that were essentially glued or sewn in as if they were never supposed to detach. These are the pieces that get yanked at over and over to come out, and when you feel like you've got a good grip and it's starting to let up, it snaps back into place as if it's never been lifted. So, how do I detach them from my picture? How do you remove something that's been in a place so long that it's developed a bond or connection with everything around it? It makes you feel like if you uproot it from its position, everything else will come crashing down. The first step is accepting the idea that everything may need to come crashing down. A 20-year-old attachment will not be easy to break, but the understanding of the severity of the problem will help you press on. If the walls of the city of Jericho could come down simply through obedience and faith in knowing that God has already won the battle, so could these generational curses.

The next piece is to recognize that God is a stronghold too! "He is my stronghold, my refuge and my savior (2 Samuel 22:3, NIV). David said this in his song of praise to the Lord as he reflected on the many battles that he faced with his enemies. The Hebrew word used in this scripture is *misgab*, and it means high tower or a rock affording shelter. David recognized that, though he may have been under consistent attack, God always provided shelter from his enemies and He made him victorious over, and over, and over again. David recognized that shelter to be a stronghold, a place that is fortified so as to protect against attack.

So, while there may be strongholds in your story that make your damaged or deteriorating pieces seem unmovable, the Lord, who is your rock and your fortress, is also the stronghold that will deliver you from the fortified attacks, just as He did for David. David inherited his stronghold in the Philistines, just as many of us have inherited ours. The war with your stronghold isn't new; it's generational. God is giving you an oppurtunity to fight and claim victory for your lineage, just like He did for David. David claimed his victory not by the works of His own hands but by his acknowledgement of his Deliverer and his Champion. Yes, he used his hands in war, but his victory always came before he even lifted finger. He yielded to God's power before each war, not advancing until God announced his victory. David didn't walk into a battle unaware of the outcome. And God didn't let him go in unarmed either.

Over the years, God had been implanting core principles in me as I kept asking what to do in these battles that I felt I was consistently in. I kept asking what the "secret sauce" was to this war that I felt was unending. *Spoiler Alert* There is no secret sauce. He is the stronghold that will demolish all strongholds, and He will arm me with what I need for the battle. He reminded me of foundational concepts that were actually my armor in the battle to destroy those generational curses. What I counted as simple, everyday things, God used in the same way that He did with David and the smooth stones that defeated Goliath, the Philistine. Don't discount the simple things God tells you. Despite how life feels, God will fight the war but He's still going to arm you with what you need for battle. He's not trying to make it hard, and He's not going to give you some algorithm that you have to try and decode to find your way out of a hard place. He will make it plain.

SUBMISSION

Submission starts with humbling yourself. This word is difficult for a lot of people, well, because…. pride. Humbling yourself, or downgrading the level control in your own life, is what allows us to submit to God's will. A practical example of what submission and humility look like is James, Jesus' brother. In his book, James shows us that humility is the way to submission. The very fact that James is the one to write the letter on humility is the perfect setup, because James did not become a believer until after Jesus' His resurrection. Jesus' own brother couldn't submit himself to the Messiahship of Christ while He was on the earth. In the book of James, we find him preaching humility but, in the book of John, while Jesus was alive and spreading the Good News, we find James and Jesus' other brothers telling Jesus to leave Galilee and go to Judea so that His disciples could see the works He did. They said that no one who wants to become a public figure acts in secret (John 7:3-4). "Not even his brothers believed in him" (John 7:5). This is the complete opposite of the humble teachings later to come in James, but this gives us an idea of James' disbelief in Jesus' Messiahship. He was in active participant in challenging Jesus with the pride of life due to disbelief. There isn't specific scripture that states the reason why James didn't belief Jesus was the Messiah, but I can imagine that it had a lot to do with the fact that they were siblings. Submitting to my sibling would be extremely hard for me to do too. I mean, would you believe if your brother or sister told you that they were the Messiah?

Then we find James, after Jesus' resurrection and before He ascends up to Heaven, now a believer. Somewhere in the 3 years of Christ's ministry, death, and resurrection James was humbled. And I know he's humbled, not just because he asks us to be humbled, but because of the way that he introduces his letter to the church. James 1:1 says "James, a servant of God and of the Lord Jesus Christ". This is his introduction to the Jewish Christian church. There were two key things that showed me his humility:

- The use of the word servant, which is by definition lowly, but lack of use of the words "Apostle", "Disciple", "Pastor," which he was. He was in fact all of these things but above all, a servant of God sent fourth to help the Jew and Gentile find their way or keep hold of what's anchoring them.

- He doesn't even mention that he's Jesus' brother. It's through research that we're able to know that the James who wrote the book of James is in fact one of Jesus' brothers, but he does not mention it once in his letter. We find out that the author James is Jesus' brother through the process of elimination with the 3 other potential James' in the New Testament, but the intentional omission of his relation to the Lord and Savior Jesus Christ and his admission to servitude of his own brother reveal humilty before the message is even preached in James 4.

So now, a humbled man is coming to teach us about humility and submission. As the example goes, "sit down, be humble." This is the ultimate example of how we must submit. Although there may be prior resistance, once you know and believe you dive all the way in with no reservation. You don't fear your past lack of submission, you simply move forward in agreement with what you know.

God taught me submission through humility. I tried to plunge forward into obedience without considering submitting myself and my will to Him. Naturally, this resulted in destruction for me. If you haven't laid down what you want so you can pick up what He has for you, the things you want will drive all of your decisions. I thought I could be obedient without submission, but submission is a prerequisite. It's the "yes" before the "yes". Submission is a necessary practice that takes away the sacrifice from obedience. You don't feel like you've lost anything because what you want is in perfect harmony with what He wants.

> **Submission is a necessary practice that takes away the sacrifice from obedience. You don't feel like you've lost anything because what you want is in perfect harmony with what He wants.**

In the last chapter, I talked about how I submerged myself into God's plan without completely submitting. This is where I learned that I can't break strongholds in my life without submitting to the way God wanted to do it. If I try, every attempt will lead to disobedience or pain. I have to be okay with following and not leading when it comes to God's plan for my life. If you re-member, I had control issues, so this was not a simple concept for me. Surrender isn't a one-step process. It's a daily decision to say yes and approaching it daily will help ease the pain of letting go of your desires. This is something I had to learn. Attempting to submit will be faced with opposition from the enemy, but it's all about who you choose to listen to and what you choose to believe.

The act of submission strips away our ill intent for the blessings we ask for and it focuses on what's good for the Kingdom. The process of submission comes at the cost of my own benefit and pleasure, because it's not about me. It's always been about Him. That's not to say that I'll never receive the things I want in this world, but Matthew 6:33 says, "seek first the Kingdom of heaven and all these things will be added to you" (NIV). When I re-focus what my intentions are and make the advancement of the kingdom my motive for all things, God will give me the desires of my heart. But when I seek the desires of my heart, I become proud and start coveting the things of this world for personal gain. At this point, it becomes excruciatingly hard to submit to the things He wants for me that are in place to advance His Kingdom.

So, what do you do when God tells you to submit yourself and your plan to Him and, out of negligence or complete disobedience, you don't? You run into the obstacle of not being able to obey God. And in keeping with the scripture that tells us "obedience is better than sacrifice," a sacrifice will need to be made. The submitting process will stretch you and press you, but it's all for your good. It may not feel like it, and it WILL feel out of place, but His plan is for your good. When you surrender your will first, you tell God (and yourself) that you're completely letting go of the things you wanted and that you'll be satisfied with whatever He has for you, knowing He only has good things in store. Your submission is presumed satisfaction with whatever He wants for you, and this is what makes obedience a characteristic.

OBEDIENCE

It's only after submission that you can truly walk in obedience, and it comes a little more naturally at this point. When God tells you to do something or refrain from something it won't go against your thoughts or your desires, because you've surrendered them to His. David did this, and it led to the defeat of his giant, his stronghold. It was a process that was curated over many years for him before and after he defeated Goliath. When it came time to take down his giant, David's submission, obedience, and consistency are what led him to victory.

So, after I took two steps back to submission, I was able to move forward to obedience. I learned that the free will God gives us is used to determine if we'll choose Him. I have a choice every time I arrive at the test, and if I didn't decide that God's will is better for me I'm never truly choosing Him. This book was an act of obedience, it was me choosing Him. I was never convinced I was a writer or that anyone would ever read what I have to say. But God told me that I needed to write about my experiences and my journey, so I did.

The cliché "take it one day at a time" began to show itself so valuable at this point in my life, because day 1 of submission is easy compared to day 100, especially if you feel like your submission has led to no fruit. Every day, I'm faced with more and more challenges and temptations that make it hard to continue to say "yes" to God. And when you look at the aggregate of days and think about more of that to come, you get overwhelmed and may feel hopeless. But, when you realize that Submission is just a daily decision that leads to obedience. Our failures today don't negate the opportunity for submission tomorrow, and it's a little easier to digest.

> **Submission is just a daily decision that leads to obedience. Our failures today don't negate the opportunity for submission tomorrow.**

The journey to obedience after submission was not consistent at all for me. Obedience became a characteristic, but I still have to submit myself and my will every day. New people, challenges, and opportunities arrive on the daily so there was no "one and done" to the surrender of my will. I didn't choose "yes" every day, but I got up every day with the heart to say "yes," regardless of my failures the previous day. And when I did fall or felt let down, disappointed, or hurt, obedience looked a lot like actually believing Romans 8:28. I learned that sometimes you just have to make a decision to believe what God says, despite your feelings. God's voice isn't like the guy from the Allstate commercial: distinct, loud, and clear. You simply have to make a choice to believe what you read, hear, and know about the nature of God and what He has planned for you. And if you don't

> **Sometimes you just have to make a decision to believe what God says, despite your feelings.**

know, it means you need to spend more time getting to know Him. His scripture will turn into a guiding voice that helps you obey. His voice may not always lead to something that feels good or looks positive in the moment, but don't forget Romans 8:28.

God's voice may be the one telling you to endure pain, but it's for your good. God's voice may be the one telling you to give up something you've worked on for years, but it's for your good. God's voice may be the one telling you to leave everything you've ever known for a place where you know nothing and no one, but it's for your good. Pain, hurt, suffering, and discomfort aren't always signs that the enemy is moving in your life. Long-suffering is a fruit of the Spirit and it's often a sign that God is tearing down walls like He did at Jericho or an opportunity for Him to show His power like He did when He raised Lazarus from the dead. So don't run from the voice that might be telling you to stay even though you want to go, or that might be saying to be alone for a while, or to leave something you've known your entire life. Long-suffering leads us to hope. Romans 5:3-5 says,

> ...but we also glory in our sufferings, because we know that suffering produces perseverance; perseverance, character; and character, hope. And hope does not put us to shame, because God's love has been poured into our hearts through the Holy Spirit, who has been given to us (NIV).

The hope that long-suffering produces will lead you through obedience and produce consistency. And not just for you, for your hearers as well (1 Timothy 4:16).

Taking it one day at a time allowed me to get to the point where I could look back and see that there was consistency in my submission and obedience. It also got me to the point where submission wasn't a decision anymore, because I lost sight of my will. I was no longer submitting to God's will but rather *existing* in God's will. I had nothing to oppose anymore, and His will for me became my will for me. And that became a consistent "yes" whenever God asked me to do something because I had no reason to say no. It became obedience.

CONSISTENCY

This is key, as the saying goes. In the beginning of my reconnection with Christ, this is what He whispered to me when I asked Him how to find Him again. I remember being so distraught because in every attempt to build my connection or know Him better, I always failed. When God told me that consistency was the first step, I immediately sought ways to be consistent: going to church every Sunday, no matter how tired I was or how comfy my bed was. Enabling the scripture for the day on my bible app was another thing. These were what I knew how to do and what I knew I could be consistent with. A few months passed with this consistency, and then we arrived at Easter Sunday, 2018 - my resurrection day. After that day, and through the journey that God has taken me on, I don't even recall the effort for consistency on my end. I believe that after my resurrection and day of Pentecost, the Holy Spirit, my Advocate, stepped in to do the work for me. The Holy Spirit is CRITICAL in tearing down strongholds, as it's the only way to truly be consistent.

It's only through the Holy Spirit that we're made free of sin and death (Romans 8:3-4). And through the Holy Spirit, we don't have to rely on our own strength to take down something that's been around for generations. The Spirit will work on your behalf to make you righteous in God's sight and to tear down the strongholds and chains on your life.

In one of my Divinity courses I was given the assignment to assess the gifts that Christ left His people when He ascended and determine which is the most underutilized. The gifts Christ left us here on this earth are His Word, His Spirit, and Community. Interestingly enough, almost my entire class wrote about how God's Word is the most underutilized gift. And while I'm of the opinion that all are drastically underutilized, I'd have to say that the Holy Spirit is at the top of the list. God's Word, God's people...all tangible. You can see it, feel it, and have a physical connection with it. The Holy Spirit is the exact opposite; people don't explore what they can't see, and it makes it hard for them to believe in it. This is why faith is so hard. Our minds start short circuiting when we're expected to believe something we can't see or that doesn't look possible. Enabling a relationship with the Holy Spirit is next level faith. Not only do you have to believe that there's a God of the universe who has created the world and everything in it and controls all life and destiny, but now, you have to believe that His Spirit is with you, living inside you to help guide you and lead you to righteousness—none of which you can actually see. The very nature of the Holy Spirit causes less exploration into that precious gift that was given to us. As a result, a lot of Christians stop at what they can see and touch. But when you're dealing with strongholds and chains, which are principalities, nothing in the earthly realm is equipped to take down demons that are not of this earthly realm. You cannot fight principalities with flesh and you simply cannot tear down strongholds in your life in your own strength. You cannot do this without the Holy Spirit.

The Holy Spirit, the Advocate, serves countless purposes for the believer. When activated and fed, He does the work necessary for us to please God, so we don't have to fight with our flesh. The Spirit does it on our behalf. And while He's fighting, He's guiding us to righteousness. He's rearranging our distorted pieces. He's dismantling our strongholds and healing the wounds they left. The Holy Spirit has the strength to tear out that piece of the puzzle that kept snapping back into place when stretched. And He's the only one who can do it.

> And so it was with me, brothers and sisters. When I came to you, I did not come with eloquence or human wisdom as I proclaimed to you the testimony about God. For I resolved to know nothing while I was with you except Jesus Christ and Him crucified. I came to you in weakness with great fear and trembling. My message and my preaching were not with wise and persuasive words, but with a demonstration of the Spirit's power, so that your faith might not rest on human wisdom, but on God's power (1 Corinthians 2:1-5, NIV).

The consistency that the Holy Spirit bred in me was not of my own works; it was extremely clear that He was working and not me. Through the Holy Spirit, who led me in consistency, generations of strongholds were demolished. The curse is broken. My children and their children don't have to bear the weight of this stronghold. God showed me that consistency was critical in the tearing down of strongholds, because your demons are persistent. You can't let your enemy show up to church more than you do. You can't let him talk to God more than you do, and you can't allow him to pursue you harder than you pursue the you that God's waiting for you to be. These acts of consistency in

> **You can't let your enemy show up to church more than you do. You can't let him talk to God more than you do, and you can't allow him to pursue you harder than you pursue the you that God's waiting for you to be.**

our lives lead to strength, they help us find hope, and they help us find direction.

Being consistent means doing somethings not because I want to but because I need to. Whatever He tells me to do…I just do it until He says stop. And I'll know when He says stop, because He won't tell me to stop one thing without giving me provision for the next.

That consistency led to my strongholds being destroyed and demolished. The last chain fell, and my soul wailed with praise. All of my pain, years of suffering and not fitting in, resistance at every door…it was all worth it. The grip that the devil has had on me and my family is gone, because the Holy Spirit was made strong in my weakness and fought for me.

I remember the day that the last chain fell off me distinctly, and I remember my soul weeping with joy. See, I never thought I'd actually arrive here because one of the other generational curses that was layered on top of all of my strongholds was laziness. And not the kind of lazy that doesn't want to do anything with their life, but the kind of lazy that's more willing to settle for where it's at than fight for the new thing. The stronghold of laziness will tell you that the work and the pain aren't worth it. It'll tell you that the promise on the other side isn't worth what you're having to endure to get there and that life's not that bad here. On top of that, reflecting on the sheer volume of all of the issues in your life just feeds the voice of laziness, making it even stronger. Dealing with generational curses from my mom's side and voids from my dad's, I realized this was no easy fight, and I simply could not do it alone. When these chains finally fell, I saw myself running this race with endurance, never getting tired of the obstacles that arise because of the value of the promise.

That's another catalyst in this journey – His promises. Write them down and look at them every single day. He cannot lie, so His promises are fact. Reminding yourself of what He told you that He has planned for you helps to combat the lies the enemy will feed you daily. Burn those lies with His truth. I clung to every last word that He told me He was going to do, and, every time I got weary, I reminded myself that it couldn't end here because God's Word hadn't come into fruition yet. Have faith in Philippians 1:6. Planting myself in His promises helped me not run back to the detrimental things that could comfort me in my time of despair. I can now look at the thing that once promised comfort and tell God, honestly, I don't need it anymore; I have a real promise. If you need an analogy, just keep your eyes fixed on the pot of gold at the end of the rainbow.

> He brought me out into a spacious place; He rescued me because He delighted in me. (2 Samuel 22:20, NIV).

God fought for me. He never stopped chasing me to guide me back to His flock. And then He showed me how to fight for myself even while I was alone and in pain. God told me I had value and, with that value, love. I was able to walk towards something. Then, He helped me see it and believe it for myself and that gave me the strength to pursue it. The Holy Spirit, in it's good and mighty strength, tore down the very things keeping me from seeing the full potential of who God made me to be. I saw all of my pieces on the table.

When you have a whole, distorted image, yes, God can multiply it, but it will replicate distortion. When you have all of your pieces that were broken by God and you give Him all you have, He will multiply those pieces through your generations as freedom from bondage.

MASTERPIECE

mas·ter·piece
/ˈmastərˌpēs/

noun

1. a work of outstanding artistry, skill, or workmanship

I am a masterpiece. I am perfection. Not because I'm perfect or because my puzzle is fully put together, but because I'm working with the right pieces now. I'm a WIP (work in progress). I'm less concerned about finishing the puzzle; I know that will happen now. My pieces are here and accounted for, and I've plucked out the pieces that had me bound to the wrong image for so long. Now the picture has the opportunity to be perfect. I am mastering my pieces.

Now that I've been fully disassembled, I look at my pieces and can't help but get excited about what God's going to do with them. If disassembly is healing, then what's re-assembly? I imagine the re-assembly process looks like God multiplying my pieces so that others can benefit from them. I've always known the lessons I was learning were in place to benefit more than just me. The ground is now tilled, and this is where my seed becomes a harvest. This is where the "more" that God is requiring isn't simply something that I can produce, but it's more of what I can sacrifice to benefit His Kingdom. It's giving my time, it's productivity, giving my talent, my love, my grace, my finances…it's giving me. I'm returning back to God and the masterpiece that He made.

I see God taking His sweet time with this work of art that He's brought back to life, and I see a picture of a worthy woman being created. Sometimes we feel like we can only share or write about things after we've completely come out of it. But the confirmation of victory is what gives us the ability to boast about sunny skies while in the storm. Your victory just may come through your testimony and this, my friends, is mine.

Ridding myself of the counterfeit pieces in my puzzle was the step I had been missing my entire life. I could never really believe that I had a promise of anything, because shame had told me that I've lost my worth. And if I have no worth, I have no hope, which makes me hold on to what I want or what I'm doing for myself because I'm the only one working for me. In order to let go of what you have and believe that God has something better for you, you have to believe that you're worth it. We lose our sense of worth through years of shame and condemnation. God didn't send that, and He doesn't want you to live there.

It's hard for us to believe that God will give us the desires of our heart because we have so many different things that we want all the time, and sometimes it feels like He won't do it for us no matter how many times we ask. But what I learned is that God wants to give us the desires of our heart if those desires and intentions are modeled after the person He wants us to be. He's not just going to frivolously start giving everybody every earthly or sinful desire they want. It's always going to be His will above ours. And the purpose of the Kingdom of God will always be priority. As you grow and learn His will for your life, your will becomes His. That's when you'll start seeing all the desires of your heart being manifested.

And if you don't know what His will for your life

is, spend more time with Him. Seek His will. And don't get weary if you don't hear what He wants immediately. I remember when I couldn't hear God's voice. I remember feeling like it had everything to do with how much sin I was in. In a sense, it did. I thought my lack of hearing His voice had to do with the fact that He didn't want to talk to me while I was in my sin. I've learned that's where He talks the most.

What I perceived as His lack of interest in me was actually my lack of interest in His will. See, God is always with us; He longs for intimacy. That means He's always wanting to talk to us, but we have to be willing and ready to listen. When we feel like we can't hear God, it's usually because we're coming to Him pushing our own agenda and not just asking Him to speak. We ask Him to change a situation or send guidance on what to do with our current relationships, but what if neither of those things are what He wants to talk about in that moment? We learn from the Bible that He doesn't speak aimlessly. It could be that He's speaking, just not to the very thing that we need answers to or the answer we want, so we're not listening. Or, it could be that He already told you what He needs from you, and you need to reflect on the last thing that God said and simply do it. Spend more time just asking for God's voice with no agenda, and He will reveal His will.

We can't just be in consistent pursuit of what we want from God while neglecting what He wants from us. When you hear from Him, be open to His breaking methods. He will send provision for whatever He's asking you to do. You just have to trust Him.

I know being open and trusting to the idea of God breaking you sounds ludicrous. Who actually desires to be broken and endure pain? It's human nature to desire mending, not intentionally breaking. But my goal is to help change your perspective on what true healing looks like. It doesn't

My goal is to help change your perspective on what true healing looks like. It doesn't start with mending, and it's not a race to perfection.

start with mending, and it's not a race to perfection.

We try to strive for perfection or as good as you can get when building something or fixing it. So, picture yourself putting together something that you bought from IKEA. The instructions are in Swedish, the pictures says you need two people to do it but you're alone and you speak English. As you set out to make this masterpiece, if you find one piece missing or you accidently break something, you'd head back to the store, right? They'll either give you the missing piece or give you an entirely new product so you can start over. That's how I felt about my life through this process. Getting to know each piece of my puzzle was brutal. It took forever and I hated uncovering those pieces of myself. It made me feel like I was just a completely jacked up human being. Every day I wanted to return it for a new, undamaged one. Every time I found something broken, missing, or stuck, I'd cry out in agony asking God to replace my life with a new one. I felt like I was sitting there with no instructions. Many times, I felt like I'd be willing to settle for something written in Swedish or picture instructions so that I knew if I was following the right guidelines.

But that's not how God works.

God is an artist. He makes beautiful pieces of work and makes no mistakes. The life that God gave each and every one of us was uniquely created and divinely organized to lead you to Him. But He wants you to come to the realization of that. He wants you to find your way to Him. As I set out to start building my life with all of the pieces laid out, God takes me on an interesting journey through my pieces. So, I'm not just putting them together to build my masterpiece, I'm exploring each one, learning why I am the way I am and who I am. This process isn't cookie cutter. My process might not be yours, but a few things hold consistent and necessary in the process: love God, love yourself, love others, and allow the Holy Spirit to work through you. And if you've not been able to do even one of those things, disassembly is required.

We have to truly trust that God knows us better than we know ourselves, because He truly does. It's such a cliché, but there are things about yourself that you don't even know yet, but God does. I didn't know that I liked history until I became an adult. I crave learning about history! When I go on vacations or visit new cities now, I HAVE to get a history lesson on the ins and outs of that place, and I have to know how that city/country came to be. I'm fascinated by it. In high school, it was just a subject that I passed. But now, I've learned that I'm a histo-

Love God, love yourself, love others, and allow the Holy Spirit to work through you. And if you've not been able to do even one of those things, disassembly is required.

ry connoisseur. Can you imagine not knowing something that simple about yourself? Now imagine the big things that you don't know about you, but God does. This is why we can't reject His methods, His placement, or His will. We don't know what God knows and we don't know how He's going to use what He knows to manifest Jeremiah 29:11.

We cannot reject His timing. We live in such an instant gratification time period that doesn't allow us to be patient. I don't know what this thing is that makes us need to be first, but I know it's not a fruit that's produced by God. Just because something comes first doesn't mean that it has authority or is glorified more than anything that comes next or last. God proved this when He created animals and all of nature first, then created man to reign over it and made man higher than it. David also proved this. His brothers were on the battle line fighting the Philistines before he ever showed up. Not only were his brothers there first, but they were also more qualified by man's standards. But by enacting everything he spent time learning and developing, David was able to defeat a giant that his brothers couldn't and then go on to become king. God chose David; He chose Adam, and He did it in His timing.

Ask yourself, Do you only trust God for the things that you want from Him? Or do you have real faith that trusts Him for the things He wants for you, even though you might not know what they are, and it may take time, pain, and discomfort?

Kirk Franklin has a song called "I am," and in the chorus he says, "I'm on my way to who I am." I don't think that anything has ever described my life so perfectly. I know who I am now, and I know Who's I am. I am not fully that person yet, but I'm on my way.

The fight is hard. It's relentless and scary. But I promise, it's so worth it. I used to only imagine myself being free from pain, shame, and unworthiness. I used to only imagine myself being able to forgive the people that hurt me. I never imagined myself liking myself, let alone loving myself. But today, I stand healed and free from the bondage of those things that I thought were simply engrained in my image. I'm so grateful. More than grateful, I'm actually in awe that God did it. I always knew that He had the power to, but when He actually does it for you, it hits different.

Loving yourself fully is possible. Freedom from past hurt or shame is possible. Only God could take something as dirty and disgusting as sexual assault and use it to His glory. There is a harvest that will come from your fight and your perseverance. Trust me, that harvest is worth it. The Jeremiah 29:11 version of you deserves your endurance, because you're worth it; Jesus proved that.

Epilogue

Not for Sale

B ecause you are now a work in progress, you are a masterpiece. The guarantee of that is in your submission to the Artist. Although you are not a finished product, you're now worth much more than you could imagine. Typically, when a masterpiece is finished, its value is assessed, and the work is put up for sale based on that value. I want to let you know that you are a masterpiece that cannot be sold. You are not for sale.

Your assessed value climbs daily because of the Artist behind the masterpiece. The more your value escalates, the more vulnerable you will be to potential buyers. The potential buyers will be people and things in the world that Satan will attempt to use to derail your purpose and purchase you. You cannot be sold—even if the full value of your masterpiece isn't recognized by you yourself, and even if your pieces still seem useless. Your pieces aren't for sale either.

After we start breaking, that's when we feel the most useless and without value. That very feeling we have is proof of our value. Satan will come into our hearts to attempt to purchase what God is trying to glorify, and he will do this at our weakest moments with whomever he needs to use to get the job done. It's in these moments that we must learn the art of standing still and waiting. The moments where we're a work in progress but have not seen the promise…that's when the bidding begins. You'll be inundated with choices that lead to temporary profit but may cause you to lose your progress. Stand still and wait, you are not for sale to the highest bidder.

In these still moments, I want to encourage you that, while you're standing still to wait on Him, you're still moving by God's inertia. What may look like standing still to man, because there's no forward progress in a decision or a sale, looks like faith to God. And faith is the substance of things hoped for. The stillness is a part of the process. We have to be still because God is the one Who's moving. We may not always see it or feel it, but He's always moving. And while He's making you a masterpiece, He's also preparing the place of your promise. That place is being handcrafted specifically for you to be exactly what you need and to house everything you need to do what He's called you to do.

God created man for worship. When God created Adam, He prepared Eden for him, ahead of him, so that the garden could be the place that man worshipped Him. God made all of the preparations for Adam to live and worship Him before He even created Adam.

In the same way that God made preparations for what Adam would use to worship Him with, before He created Adam, God is making preparations for your place of promise before bringing you there. He's going before you and planting the things you need to bring Him honor so that, when you arrive, all you have to do is till by simply worshiping. Genesis 2:8 tells us that before man was created, God made Eden; He created the garden. The garden was simply a fenced in area with trees in it, created for protection.

He arranged all of the necessary pieces for worship to come forward through man before putting man in the place he created for Him. This is what He does for us in our waiting seasons. While we're being still, and it feels like nothing is happening, God is making broad brush strokes on the canvas that you'll only see once you get there. This is where faith is built, and it's where faith is tested the most. This place will feel like purgatory at times, and it's because you have bidders left and right, attempting to purchase this beautiful work in progress. For you, it'll just look like comfort or peace. Typically, your bidders know of your value before you do. And every oppurtunity he gets, Satan sends a bidder to steal you away from worship and stillness and pull you back into his plan. He does this here because he knows how impatient we are, he knows how fragile we are, and he knows what God is doing. Waiting is HARD. Denying the temptations that feel like they'll comfort you in your waiting is even harder. But again, when you know what you're up against, it allows you to fight with the right weapons.

When I became the work in progress that I am, a masterpiece, I really was a new person. I saw God in a new way. I saw me in a new way and, little by little, He started revealing what I was created for. It was a beautiful thing, really. But it did not mean that sin and temptation just magically left my life. And it did not mean I had arrived at my promise. I was still waiting on God to come through on the things He promised me while still rebuilding my puzzle.

I got my nose pierced just after my 29th birthday. Anyone who's ever had a nose piercing knows about the dreaded bump but, for anyone who doesn't know, it's pretty typical to get one right on your piercing a few weeks after it's done. And yes, it's pretty gross. Now, I'm not one who typically gets facial blemishes so the idea of that eye sore just sitting on my face, right on the new piercing that everyone is naturally looking at, gave me all kinds of anxiety. It had to go. I went back to the tattoo parlor about a month after I got the piercing, attempting to convince them that I was allergic to the material they used and that I needed more premium material. After obliging my request and putting titanium in my nose instead of surgical steel, the piercer gave me some very specific instructions. She said, "clean it twice, daily, and apply pressure." She said that pressure was the most important part because it would ensure that the bump didn't fill back up with fluids. After just 2 days of doing this consistently, the bump went away.

> **❝ Clean it twice, daily, and apply pressure. ❞**

Satan saw my value on the rise and, as it's in his nature, sent the highest bidder to buy me back into his plan. He does this by way of picking at the wounds that aren't open any more but are still healing. My abandonment issues, the fact that I didn't love myself before; he will find the things that used to be your weakness and exploit them because he knows that it's still a scab. The difference between something that you're healed from vs healing from is the difference between a scar and a scab. A scab can be reopened, a scar can't. So, he'll find the scabs and pick at them during this waiting season, just looking for the right thing that you're willing to re-open, and boy, I had a TON of scabs. My piercer's instructions rang like the voice of God during this time. "Clean it twice, daily, and apply pressure." As the healing process goes for any wound, we have to take care of it, especially when there are so many opportunities for it to open back up.

Cleansing your wound, twice daily, means that you have to be intentional about cleansing yourself from your impurities and feeding yourself with truth however many times a day that needs to happen for you. We're fed lies all . . . day . . . long. At some point, your healing wounds are going to be susceptible to those lies and may even believe them. This is why feeding ourselves with truth is so critical. We cannot allow days to go by without pouring into our spirit what the enemy is fighting so hard to block out. We also cannot allow days to go by without cleaning. Sin is inevitable; we're born into it. God knows we're going to sin, and He knows we're going to slip up. Repentance is a gift He gave us for that should be intentional, daily. Cleanse yourself of the mistakes you've made each day so that the dirt from sin doesn't cake up on your wound and cause infection. Or worse, open it back up.

Applying pressure is God's job. You just need to be cognizant of the fact that He's allowing it to happen. The pressure is there to ensure your wound doesn't fill back up with those nasty fluids or old habits. Nothing happens outside of the will of God, so if you're being tempted and tested by the enemy, it's because God allowed it to happen. You have to recognize the season that you're in; embrace and withstand the pressure because it's a part of the healing. When you stand against the pressure, it forces out the little influences that come in to try to distort and pervert your healing. You can't get lost in this part of the process as so many people do, because that's all it is: a part of the process. It's intended to close the wound fully, to make the scab nothing but a scar.

I know it's easier said than done but be strong and

be courageous; God is still with you. Cleanse twice, daily, and apply pressure. Wait on God. If for nothing else, do it because He waited for you.

ABOUT THE
AUTHOR

Like many, Tyeisha grew up an outcast. After graduating High School in Maryland, she moved to Charlotte, NC for college. Tyeisha received her undergrad degree in Communications from Johnson C. Smith University and master's degree in Theological Studies from Liberty University. It took 26 years for Tyeisha to accept the outcast in her but once she finally embraced what God loved from the beginning, her ministry began. Tyeisha has always felt the need to pour out into others what God has poured into her, and she hopes that every fruit of her hand would be a seed planted into someone else and utilized for the glory of God.